THE STRESS

JOANNA GUTMANN establ
tancy ten years ago, concentrat
skills. She runs a variety of cours
covering a broad range of subjec   ....ntation and
assertiveness skills to communication skills, telephone
techniques and business letter and report writing.

Joanna is experienced in helping people present themselves in a professional manner, whilst retaining their
individual character.

Overcoming Common Problems Series

For a full list of titles please contact
Sheldon Press, Marylebone Road, London NW1 4DU

Overcoming Common Problems Series

Coping with Thyroid Problems
DR JOAN GOMEZ

Coping with Thrush
CAROLINE CLAYTON

Coping with Your Cervical Smear
KAREN EVENNETT

Crunch Points for Couples
JULIA COLE

Curing Arthritis Exercise Book
MARGARET HILLS AND JANET
HORWOOD

Curing Arthritis Diet Book
MARGARET HILLS

Curing Arthritis – The Drug-Free Way
MARGARET HILLS

Curing Arthritis
More ways to a drug-free life
MARGARET HILLS

Depression
DR PAUL HAUCK

Divorce and Separation
Every woman's guide to a new life
ANGELA WILLANS

**Everything Parents Should Know About
Drugs**
SARAH LAWSON

Feverfew
DR STEWART JOHNSON

Gambling – A Family Affair
ANGELA WILLANS

Garlic
KAREN EVENNETT

Good Stress Guide, The
MARY HARTLEY

Heart Attacks – Prevent and Survive
DR TOM SMITH

**Helping Children Cope with Attention
Deficit Disorder**
DR PATRICIA GILBERT

Helping Children Cope with Bullying
SARAH LAWSON

Helping Children Cope with Divorce
ROSEMARY WELLS

Helping Children Cope with Dyslexia
SALLY RAYMOND

Helping Children Cope with Grief
ROSEMARY WELLS

Hold Your Head Up High
DR PAUL HAUCK

How to Be Your Own Best Friend
DR PAUL HAUCK

How to Cope when the Going Gets Tough
DR WINDY DRYDEN AND JACK
GORDON

How to Cope with Anaemia
DR JOAN GOMEZ

How to Cope with Bulimia
DR JOAN GOMEZ

How to Cope with Difficult Parents
DR WINDY DRYDEN AND JACK
GORDON

How to Cope with Difficult People
ALAN HOUEL WITH CHRISTIAN
GODEFROY

**How to Cope with People who Drive you
Crazy**
DR PAUL HAUCK

How to Cope with Splitting Up
VERA PEIFFER

How to Cope with Stress
DR PETER TYRER

How to Enjoy Your Retirement
VICKY MAUD

How to Improve Your Confidence
DR KENNETH HAMBLY

How to Interview and Be Interviewed
MICHELE BROWN AND GYLES
BRANDRETH

How to Keep Your Cholesterol in Check
DR ROBERT POVEY

How to Love and Be Loved
DR PAUL HAUCK

How to Pass Your Driving Test
DONALD RIDLAND

How to Stand up for Yourself
DR PAUL HAUCK

**How to Start a Conversation and Make
Friends**
DON GABOR

How to Stick to a Diet
DEBORAH STEINBERG AND
DR WINDY DRYDEN

How to Stop Worrying
DR FRANK TALLIS

How to Untangle Your Emotional Knots
DR WINDY DRYDEN AND JACK
GORDON

How to Write a Successful CV
JOANNA GUTMANN

Overcoming Common Problems Series

Hysterectomy
SUZIE HAYMAN

The Incredible Sulk
DR WINDY DRYDEN

The Irritable Bowel Diet Book
ROSEMARY NICOL

The Irritable Bowel Stress Book
ROSEMARY NICOL

Is HRT Right for You?
DR ANNE MacGREGOR

Jealousy
DR PAUL HAUCK

Learning to Live with Multiple Sclerosis
DR ROBERT POVEY, ROBIN DOWIE
AND GILLIAN PRETT

Living with Angina
DR TOM SMITH

Living with Asthma
DR ROBERT YOUNGSON

Living with Diabetes
DR JOAN GOMEZ

Living with Grief
DR TONY LAKE

Living with High Blood Pressure
DR TOM SMITH

Living with a Stoma
DR CRAIG WHITE

Making the Most of Yourself
GILL FOX AND SHEILA DAINOW

Menopause
RAEWYN MACKENZIE

Migraine Diet Book, The
SUE DYSON

Motor Neurone Disease – A Family Affair
DR DAVID OLIVER

The Nervous Person's Companion
DR KENNETH HAMBLY

Out of Work – A Family Affair
ANNE LOVELL

Overcoming Anger
DR WINDY DRYDEN

Overcoming Shame
DR WINDY DRYDEN

Overcoming Stress
DR VERNON COLEMAN

The Parkinson's Disease Handbook
DR RICHARD GODWIN-AUSTEN

The PMS Diet Book
KAREN EVENNETT

Second Time Around
ANNE LOVELL

Serious Mental Illness – A Family Affair
GWEN HOWE

Sex & Relationships
ROSEMARY STONES

Stress Workbook, The
JOANNA GUTMANN

Subfertility Handbook, The
VIRGINIA IRONSIDE AND SARAH
BIGGS

Talking About Anorexia
How to cope with life without starving
MAROUSHKA MONRO

Ten Steps to Positive Living
DR WINDY DRYDEN

Think Your Way to Happiness
DR WINDY DRYDEN AND JACK
GORDON

**Understanding Obsessions and
Compulsions**
A self-help manual
DR FRANK TALLIS

Understanding Your Personality
Myers-Briggs and more
PATRICIA HEDGES

Overcoming Common Problems

The Stress Workbook

Joanna Gutmann

First published in Great Britain in 1998 by
Sheldon Press, SPCK, Marylebone Road, London NW1 4DU

British Library Cataloguing-in-Publication Data
A catalogue for this book is available from the British Library

ISBN 0–85969–787–8

Photoset by Deltatype Limited, Birkenhead, Merseyside
Printed in Great Britain by
Biddles Ltd, Guildford and King's Lynn

Contents

To Mike, Max and Toby

Introduction

Since you have picked up this book, it is reasonable to assume that you are feeling stressed. Broadly speaking, there are two forms of stress: one is the effect of major events in your life (e.g. redundancy, a house move, bereavement). This is called *specific stress*. The other type, *general stress*, is a result of a build-up of pressure in your life (often as a result of trying to fit an unreasonable amount into your day, combining the various demands of job and family, or dealing with difficult circumstances such as caring for an elderly relative). This book is primarily concerned with general stress, and its aim is to help you remove some of the pressures in your life, and to cope better with the ones that remain.

The particular aspect that this book addresses is the stress caused by the combined pressures of work and home. For every person whose day runs smoothly as a result of a supportive family and efficient childcare, there are hundreds more who feel they are doing far more than their share. It is not easy keeping the home and family running efficiently as well as working. If you combine this with the pressure to be professional at work, supportive to your partner, a loving parent to your children and a listening ear to your friends, then it is no wonder that we feel we are buckling under the strain – that is, feeling stressed.

First, consider the following. There are only two ways to ensure that stress does not ruin your life:

---

reduce the amount of stress

or

increase your ability to deal with it

Stress is a term that is frequently used to describe a feeling of being driven, never having enough time, and experiencing conflicting demands that seem to be pulling you in different directions. This feeling, combined with the inevitable tiredness, leaves us sure that there must be a better way, but uncertain as to what it is or how to achieve it.

No one can tell you what the better way is. Inevitably, individuals want different things, and only you can decide what is important to you. This book gives you the structure to discover what your priorities are. You will also find many useful ideas, together with the means to apply them to your life, and help in implementing those ideas that interest you.

Why a workbook?

A workbook is a combination of textbook and self-study pack, and its design enables you to consider the subject being dealt with by giving particular emphasis to you and your situation. Rather than simply being told what to do, you have the chance to apply the ideas through exercises, to consider alternatives, and to plan a way forward – all in a way that is relevant to you.

Using the book

This book requires a dual investment from you. You have probably already invested money in its purchase, and this money will be wasted if you don't now invest *time*. Just as you can invest money to earn interest, you can invest time. In order to gain interest on your savings you have to do without the cash today, and instead leave the money in the bank or building society. Likewise, you can put some time aside to think, plan, teach others or learn new techniques – but, as with the financial investment analogy, you will have to forgo time spent on other things, although you will gain in the longer term.

Take the time to work through each section in the book in detail and complete the exercises. In other words, try to make a proper investment in each in order to get a maximum return. Make the effort to *learn*, rather than reading the book as if it were simply a novel or newspaper. Reading to learn involves reading at a slower pace, in a more considered style, pausing to consider which points are relevant to you (or not) and why, and to make notes where necessary.

Learning also involves working through the exercises, taking the trouble to consider your responses, and then writing them down. A quick glance at the exercises does not achieve the same thing!

It is essential that you are honest with yourself as you work through the book. Therefore if you do not want anyone else to know your feelings and thoughts, keep the book hidden and work on it when you are alone. Also, spend some time asking yourself the reason for this need for privacy; is this in itself adding to your stress level?

A workbook is meant to be written in, and you will gain so much more if you take the trouble to 'personalize' it through your notes.

Structure of the book

The book is divided into five parts. After this Introduction, and the explanation of stress in Chapter 1, you will be helped to evaluate your lifestyle in terms of the demands made upon you, your strengths and weaknesses, and the immediate future you face. After that, it's time to start acting positively to reduce the stress in your life, and to develop your ability to cope with remaining stresses. This is done by eliminating things that drain your energy (e.g. worry and guilt), streamlining your day, and then building up your stamina to cope with all that life throws at you. The final chapter, Chapter 17, draws together all the parts of the book into a plan for the next few months that you can update as and when necessary.

TEXT

Each part is concerned with a particular aspect of stress or its prevention, and this type of stress is explained, together with suggested techniques for coping with it. You should read through these techniques carefully as they form the basis for the exercises and action plans that follow. The text is generally divided into small sections so that you can work through it in one sitting.

EXAMPLES

Examples are given to help make the text clear and relevant, and these are taken from a wide range of situations: some you will be able to identify with easily; others may be irrelevant to you (e.g. caring for an elderly relative when you are not in this position). Where an example is relevant, compare it to your situation; where it is not, you may find that it helps to replace it with one that is more applicable to you.

EXERCISES

The exercises are there to enable you to think about the theory in a way that is relevant to you. Usually, they are a series of questions for you to consider. There are seldom any right or wrong answers as such, but your responses will form part of the action plan you will be creating to help you cope with stress in a more positive way. Space is obviously limited within the book. Where you need more room, just copy the exercise onto a piece of paper and use that.

PUTTING IT INTO PERSPECTIVE

These short sections encourage you to take time out for reflection: to consider what you have written, to add general points, make notes, and so on. You will sometimes find that something becomes blindingly obvious once you stop to think about it, and these sections are intended as places to note this, together with anything else that *you* think is relevant.

These sections have the added benefit of encouraging you to sit back and think about more general issues in a day that is usually filled with specific problems, deadlines and so on.

POSITIVE STEPS FOR PROGRESS

These action-planning sections are designed to assist you in taking the initial steps towards reducing your stress level. They are short, and focus on one aspect only. This makes them easier to complete and, as you will find in the final section, they help you take practical steps both in the short term and the long term.

Relevance to you

Even without the constraints of political correctness, it is not possible to make a book 100 per cent relevant to every reader. For example, you may be female or male, married or not, have children or not, and so on. If any part of the book is completely irrelevant to you, simply miss it out – but, before you do, check that there is not a parallel situation that you should consider. It may be that you do not have children, but perhaps you lavish extreme care on a couple of dogs? You will gain far more from twisting a point relating to children in order to apply it to your dogs, than from ignoring the point altogether.

1
Stress

What is stress?

Stress is a particular person's response to pressure in their lives. It can be short-term or immediate pressure (e.g. a difficult interview this afternoon), or it can simply be the accumulation of many, less daunting pressures. Such pressures can come from any number of sources, but the most common ones are as follows:

- Trying to do more than is possible within the time available.
- Ongoing problems or concerns (e.g. caring for a relative, marital problems, financial difficulties).
- Your *perception* of an imbalance between demand and ability. In other words, if you feel that you do not have the ability to meet the demands made on you, the pressure will build up. Less obviously, if you feel that your ability *exceeds* the demands made on you, you will become bored and frustrated – which is also a pressure.
- Lack of control over what happens in your life. If choices and decisions are made for you, your powerlessness will be a major source of stress.

Stress is the response when the level of pressure becomes too great to tolerate, and that level is individual. It depends on what type of person you are, your current health and state of mind, and how you *perceive* a situation – rather than on the situation itself. For example, imagine that you have been asked to organize a team entering a local half-marathon to raise money for charity:

You are likely to feel positive if:	You are likely to feel negative if:
• you are the type of person who loves a challenge and learning new things	• you hate doing things that are new
• you do not have too much work on at the moment	• you are snowed under with work
• you are feeling fit and healthy and good about yourself	• you feel sluggish and a bit down

5

Your feelings about the task will be influenced by the comparative strength of the factors above. It may be that you usually thrive on challenges, but at present are recovering from flu and are particularly busy at work. Depending on the strength of the above factors, you may find that this task is just the lift you need – or, conversely, the final straw. In other words, your attitude to everything you do depends on your personality, combined with the other things required of you, and thus will vary according to individual circumstances. Stress occurs when the pressure becomes too great for *you*.

The body's response to stress

The body's immediate response to stress is physical: adrenaline and glucose are released, the digestive system shuts down, and the heart pumps blood to the essential organs and muscles (what is known as the 'fight or flight response'). This is useful when facing an immediate and serious stressor (e.g. a potential attacker), but is little help when the cause of stress is the threat of redundancies to be announced next week.

The short-term fight or flight response, though, does not last long and, provided that the body returns to normal, it presents no problem. However, if you face *ongoing* stressful situations, your body may be in almost continuous fight or flight mode, and ultimately its resources will become depleted.

If the stress continues, this depletion of your resources will leave you vulnerable to illness. Chronic stress lowers the resistance of your immune system, and is associated with a range of problems from headaches through to heart disease.

Stress also affects your behaviour and mood

BEHAVIOUR EFFECTS

When you are stressed, you are likely to withdraw into yourself, focusing on the problems you face. You are also likely to become short-tempered, often irrationally so. Voice tone will often give you away, and you may sound irritable, impatient and sharp. Also, concentration is often impaired, and there is a tendency to flit ineffectively from one task to another, possibly not completing anything.

MOOD EFFECTS

Stress makes you feel anxious, overwhelmed, unable to cope or keep up, and sometimes leaves you with an attitude of 'I can't do this, so I may as well not ever try'. This mood results in a sense of failure, and the skills and abilities of others start to seem much greater than our own. Stress can also make you feel sad, negative and full of worry. General stress can be a depressing cycle (see Figure 1).

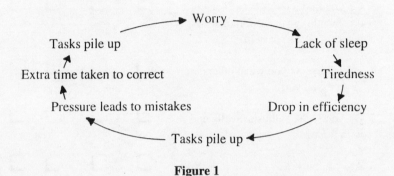

Figure 1

Some forms of stress can be the result of a major event (e.g. a change of job, illness/bereavement in the family, a major addition to your workload). Today, though, another common cause of stress is the effect of striving to *do* everything and *be* everything. The pressures caused by trying to be a good parent, partner, relation, worker, friend, etc. can mean that you constantly exist in a state of tension and eventually reach a point where you tip over into the condition known as stress.

> *EXERCISE*

Are you prone to stress?

Consider the ten questions below and answer somewhere on the scale from ALWAYS down to NEVER (if the point does not apply to you):

STRESS

	ALWAYS			NEVER
	4	3	2	1
1 Do you rush from one thing to the next?	☐	☐	☐	☐
2 Do you do several things at once?	☐	☐	☐	☐
3 Do you find it quicker and easier to do something yourself, rather than delegate or ask for help?	☐	☐	☐	☐
4 Does it irritate you when others are slower than you?	☐	☐	☐	☐
5 Do you speak enthusiastically and with force?	☐	☐	☐	☐
6 Are you tense?	☐	☐	☐	☐
7 If you take time out to relax, do you feel guilty?	☐	☐	☐	☐
8 Are you concerned that your house/car/ job/latest piece of work is as good as, or better, than other people's?	☐	☐	☐	☐
9 Do you lose your temper – or *feel* like doing so?	☐	☐	☐	☐
10 Do other people's shortcomings annoy you?	☐	☐	☐	☐

Now look back over your answers, concentrating on the pattern of the ticks. The further to the left they are (towards ALWAYS), the more prone to stress you are. Stress experts divide people into two broad categories. So-called 'Type A' characters will have most ticks in boxes 3 and 4, whereas the more laid-back 'Type B' characters will have more ticks in boxes 1 and 2.

Now compare the first hour in a typical day for Annie and Belinda – two sisters who both have a daughter and son at primary school.

Annie leaves the house at 8.20 in the mornings. As always, she is on time and both children are asking what she has packed for their break. She fumes as she joins the inevitable traffic jam, wishing the school offered a 'before school' club so that she could leave earlier and avoid the slow crawl. The children jump out at the school gate and head off to start their day as Annie forces her way back into the traffic and, thanks to some sharp lane-changing, manages to arrive at work at nine o'clock.

Annie needs to see Brian before a meeting later that morning, and is furious that he is not around as his car is in the car park. She leaves a note asking him to ring her as soon as he arrives. However, she is pleased to find Adrian at his desk and quickly explains what she needs for the presentation tomorrow.

As she runs downstairs, Annie mentally lists the three things she must do immediately, and then glares at Brian's car – hoping he hasn't rung while she was talking to Adrian. She rings his extension before she starts on the first task, and insists that his secretary ensures that he sees her note as soon as he arrives.

Belinda also leaves at 8.20 in the mornings, happy that she is within the five minutes' tolerance for getting to school on time. She resignedly raises an eyebrow at the length of the traffic jam and listens to the children's chatter as she crawls along. She parks across the road from the school and sees the children in, wishing them a happy day before turning back to her car and the drive to the office.

She lets a couple of cars into the traffic queue and ignores the hoot of impatience from the driver behind. She is parked and in the office by 9.10 and is glad that she arranged an unofficial flexitime system with her manager.

Belinda needs to see Barry first thing and rings to see if he is in. He is not, and she explains to his secretary her need to talk to him before 10.30. His secretary promises Belinda that she will get him to ring back, and then Belinda puts her papers to one side to wait for his call.

She then sorts her pile of post into important items and junk mail, and settles down with a cup of coffee to read through the letters that matter.

Annie, the 'Type A', is far more likely to be affected by stress than Belinda, 'Type B', who has a more relaxed attitude. Belinda may not get as far as

9

Annie, but she is likely to be happier and better able to cope with the stresses of her life.

EXERCISE

How do you respond to stress?

Consider what you do during an average week: think about all aspects from waking up and getting dressed in the morning, through your day, your evening, and until you fall into bed at night (and even after that!).

In the *first column* of Figure 2, list the things that cause you to feel stressed, including both the major ones (e.g. a significant event at work) and the minor things (e.g. the tube of toothpaste without a top, or lack of help in clearing the table after a meal).

When you have completed the list, turn your attention to the second and third columns. In the *second column* note how these stressors make you feel (this might be anything from irritated to murderous, from tearful to sulky, to the temptation to walk out).

What makes me stressed?	How do I feel?	What do I tend to do?

Figure 2

In the *third column*, consider how you *typically* respond (e.g. slamming the door; saying nothing; by carrying on working (but resentfully); shouting).

PUTTING IT INTO PERSPECTIVE

Consider the responses you made in Figure 2:

- Are your stressors major or minor?
- Is there a pattern?
- Do you respond differently at home and at work, or with different people?
- Are your responses generally positive or negative (are you acting to tackle or reduce the stress, or are you in fact adding to its effect through your reaction)?
- Where are you reacting to stress positively?

Note your comments on these, together with any general thoughts:

_____

_____

_____

_____

_____

_____

_____

_____

_____

_____

_____

If you can already see changes you can make, note them in 'positive steps for progress' below.

POSITIVE STEPS FOR PROGRESS

I can improve my response to situations I find stressful by:

1 _____

_____

_____

_____

_____

_____

_____

2 _____

_____

_____

_____

_____

_____

_____

3 _____

_____

_____

_____

_____

_____

_____

PART 1: EVALUATION

Before you can address the issues that cause you stress, you need to know what they are. The four chapters in Part 1 are designed to help you define your stressors through considering:

- the demands placed on you by yourself and others;
- how you would like to live your life, given the constraints you have;
- your strengths and weaknesses in terms of coping with all that you have to do;
- the things that you will have to cope with over the next few months.

In addition to focusing on your stressors, these chapters give you 'time out' simply to think and to concentrate on yourself.

2

Who am I, where am I?

As the first stage in evaluating your situation, work through the questions below, answering them as honestly as possible. They concern the demands on your time, physical and mental energy made by others.

The questions are divided into 'Tasks', 'Relationships' and 'Attitudes'. *Tasks* concentrates on what you do, both for yourself and for others, at home and at work. *Relationships* focuses on the connections between you and the people you live and work with. *Attitudes* deals with your feelings towards the demands made on you by others.

If any of the sections in this chapter are irrelevant to you, then simply put a line through them; and if there is another section that should be added for you, put it in where appropriate.

Take the time to consider and fill in each section in detail. If you rush and only give a couple of examples for each, you will not get a complete picture.

Do not judge yourself at this stage and don't bend or conceal the truth – you are only deceiving yourself, which will probably add to your stress level!

Tasks

Concentrate first on the tasks you do (e.g. washing, driving, typing).

What do I do for my spouse/partner? _____

_____

_____

_____

What do I do for my children? _____

_____

_____

_____

_____

_____

What do I do for my family and my partner's family? _____

_____

_____

What do I do for others I care for (e.g. an elderly relative)? _____

_____

_____

_____

What do I do in my home? _____

_____

_____

_____

What do I do at work? _____

_____

_____

_____

What else do I do (e.g. charity work)? _____

_____

_____

What do I do for friends? _____

_____

_____

What do I do for me? _____

_____

_____

Any others? _____

_____

_____

Relationships

How would you describe your relationship with each person/group? Don't worry about finding precise or clever words, or writing full sentences. Just make notes to give an indication of each relationship.

Spouse/partner: _____

_____

Child(ren): _____

_____

Other family: _____

_____

Work colleagues: _____

_____

Friends: _____

_____

Any others? _____

_____

Attitudes

How would you describe your attitude to the demands on your time, mental and physical energy, made by each of the following? Again, just make notes in a form that makes sense to you.

Spouse/partner: _____

_____

Children: _____

_____

Family: _____

_____

Work: _____

_____

Other commitments: _____

_____

Friends: _____

_____

Me: _____

_____

EXERCISE

Summarize the outcome

List the people or groups that you have included in these sections (e.g. partner, children, colleagues, etc.) in the first column of Figure 4. Figure 3 is an example of a filled-in summary form.

Person/group	Summary of my relationship with that person/group
Children	Although I cannot spend as much time with my children as I would wish, we have a lot of fun when we do things together.
Colleagues	We get on well on the surface, but I resent the fact that everyone assumes I will help them despite my workload. I don't feel part of the team.
Husband	I would describe our marriage as happy, but I end up doing all the household chores, even though we both work. I resent this.

Figure 3

18

For each one, look at what you have written for that person/group in the three areas (Tasks, Relationships, Attitudes), and then briefly summarize your relationship with them in column two of Figure 4.

Person/group	Summary of my relationship with that person/group

Figure 4

19

EXERCISE

From another perspective

You might wish to look at your attitude from another perspective. Think about the following questions:

What is your mood when:

you wake in the morning? _____

_____

Why? _____

_____

you are on the way to work? _____

_____

Why? _____

_____

you are on your way home? _____

_____

Why? _____

_____

Are there any other occasions that typically make you feel very positive or negative?

Positive   Negative

_____

_____

_____

_____

_____

PUTTING IT INTO PERSPECTIVE

Re-read your notes in this section and consider the areas where your feelings are positive and negative. If you want to write anything down to consolidate your thoughts or remind yourself of something, here's a space:

_____

_____

_____

_____

_____

_____

_____

_____

_____

_____

_____

3
Where do I want to be?

In the last chapter, you looked at the demands on yourself and your time. Now look at the same issues from a different perspective. Answer the following questions honestly and realistically:

How would I like my spouse/partner to describe me to a colleague? ____

_____

_____

_____

How would I like them to describe our relationship? _____

_____

_____

_____

I would like our relationship to be: _____

_____

_____

_____

How would I like my children to describe me to their friends? _____

_____

_____

_____

I would like my relationship with my children to be: _____

_____

_____

_____

WHERE DO I WANT TO BE?

How would I like my family to describe me? _____

_____

_____

_____

What would I like my friends to say about me? _____

_____

_____

_____

What do I want my home to be like? _____

_____

_____

_____

From my job I want (apart from money!): _____

_____

_____

_____

What would I do with time each week that *had* to be spent on me?

_____

_____

_____

_____

EXERCISE

Far from ideal, or not so bad really?

Look back over your answers to questions in this chapter and the previous
one, and consider the areas where there is a significant difference between

where you are now and where you want to be. Make notes in Figure 5 of any general ideas as to what is preventing you from being where you want to be (and anything else you want to highlight as important).

Areas where there is a difference between where I am and where I want to be	Why is there such a difference?	What is the effect on me?

Figure 5

The middle column of Figure 5 may highlight specific problems with people or workload, or vague reasons such as 'unrealistic hopes', 'never quite get time', etc. Once you have completed this section on evaluation, you will find that the remainder of the book will assist you to reduce the amount of stress you face and to increase your ability to cope with remaining stress. This should help you get nearer to the 'standards' you have outlined in this chapter.

4

Where I'm strong – and where I wobble!

It is easy to dwell on our weak areas, failures and the negative things we face, but doing this – not surprisingly – only adds to feelings of stress.

The purpose of this chapter is to help you take a balanced look at your strengths and weaknesses in order to give you confidence in your abilities, to highlight areas where you need to develop, and to help you gain additional skills in order to cope.

This is intended to be a 'snapshot' of you today; do not dwell on the past or on anything too remote in the future. In the *strengths* column of Figure 6, identify the positive aspects of your personality – skills and things you do well at home and at work. Do not leave things out because you feel they are irrelevant or too insignificant to matter.

Strengths	Weaknesses
E.g. Talking to customers. Coping with son's vegetarian diet. Village Hall committee.	*E.g.* Tend to be late. Can't keep up with the ironing. Computer Skills.

Figure 6

25

In the *weaknesses* column, identify any aspects of your personality of which you are not so proud, together with any areas where you feel you are less successful and lack the skills you would like or need. Be realistic, honest and balanced (try to give a strength for every weakness).

You may find it helpful to divide the chart into areas such as work, home, children, marriage, etc. The top half of Figure 6 gives you some examples.

Look at the items in your strengths column, and spend a few minutes taking pride in them. To be assured of your skills boosts your self-confidence and can help you use them to best effect. On those days when you feel useless, just return to this list for an immediate lift!

POSITIVE STEPS FOR PROGRESS

For each entry in the weaknesses column in Figure 6, decide to what extent it matters. Are you being unrealistic in trying to be perfect, or is this an area

---

1 *Never say 'no' to anything at work.*

Why a weakness? *I take on more than I can get through. I waste time resenting what I am being expected to do.*

Making a start on change:

a *Decide on example words to use when saying 'no' and practise them so they sound familiar when I do it for real.*

b *Listen to what I am asked to do and decide whether I want to say 'no' completely, or 'not now/not by that deadline'.*

c *On Monday, say 'no' to something simple - like 'do you want a coffee?'*

(See Chapter 14 for help with saying 'no'.)

Figure 7

where change would have a positive impact on your life? Cross out the entries that are merely an attempt at perfection and, from those that remain, bracket any that naturally fall together (e.g. never say 'no' to anything at work, and always go along with what my husband wants to do). Now list the three most important things below, and then identify three small steps ((a) to (c)) you could take to achieve change. Do not try to reach perfection at once or to take unrealistically large steps. An example entry is provided in Figure 7.

Weaker areas to work on:

1 _____

Why a weakness? _____

_____

_____

Making a start on change:

a _____

_____

_____

b _____

_____

_____

c _____

_____

_____

2 _____

Why a weakness?_____

_____

_____

Making a start on change:

a _____

_____

_____

b _____

_____

_____

c _____

_____

_____

3 _____

Why a weakness?_____

_____

_____

Making a start on change:

a _____

_____

_____

b _____

_____

_____

c _____

_____

_____

Techniques for overcoming areas where you feel less able or confident are given throughout the remainder of the book. As you work through it, use the 'positive steps for progress' sections to help you implement change.

5

What's around the corner?

Lack of time sometimes causes us to rush from one thing to the next, looking only as far as the coming week, or even a day or so ahead. This short-term outlook means that planning is a non-starter, and events that we dread loom as an ill-defined black cloud on the horizon.

If you can take a structured look at the coming six months, you can actively prepare for what you will have to do, quantify your worries, enjoy anticipation of the good things, and spread your workload as sensibly as possible.

$$\boxed{EXERCISE}$$

What's next?

Make a list in Figure 8 of anything and everything that you anticipate will happen over the next six months (cover a longer or shorter period if you prefer). Include any event that is not a run-of-the-mill activity, or anything that takes a lot of planning/preparation – or which you are particularly looking forward to or dreading.

Divide the list into the two categories of 'planned' (for those things that you know will happen and when) – e.g. child starting a new school – and 'might happen' for things that are a strong possibility – e.g. change of manager at work.

When you have completed your list, go back over it and put a plus sign (+) by those items you feel positive and enthusiastic about. Do not be influenced by how you *should* feel; just concentrate on how you *do* feel. Transfer these positive events to Figure 9. Spend some time thinking about why you are looking forward to these events, and list your reasons for each.

Do these events that you feel positive about have anything in common? For example, are they all things you have done before? Do they involve a

Six months from (today): _____ to: _____

Planned	Might happen

Figure 8

I feel positive about	I feel this way because

Figure 9

WHAT'S AROUND THE CORNER?

particular group of people or activity? Are they concerned with home or with work? Summarize any common themes below:

I tend to feel positive about events that: _____

_____

_____

_____

_____

_____

_____

_____

Return to your list of things that are around the corner (Figure 8) and mark with a minus sign (–) the things that you feel negative, worried or unenthusiastic about, and list them in Figure 10. Again, spend some time considering why you feel so negative about them. Is there a pattern?

I feel negative about	I feel this way because

Figure 10

31

I tend to feel negative about events that: _____

_____

_____

_____

_____

_____

_____

_____

_____

Do not be surprised if some of the things you feel less than enthusiastic about are meant to be 'good' things – for example, a holiday. Although most of us look forward to a week or two away, you can dread it as it approaches and you start thinking about the packing, sorting out cover at work and anticipating the pile of jobs when you return, trying to buy the perfect swimsuit, and so on.

Often, just acknowledging your dread can help you clarify what it is that is causing the problem, and once it's confronted it does not seem so bad. Chapter 7 will help you with this.

Try to take this 'snapshot' of the coming half-year every three months or so. Apart from reducing the pressure caused by worry, you will be able to plan what you are going to do about each event and take steps to make the positive items even better. More importantly, you will reduce the stress caused by those things you are not looking forward to (or have mixed feelings about) because your feelings will be quantified and plans can be made. Chapters 10, 11 and 14 also offer specific help with this.

There are some stressors that are a complete waste of both time and energy – things that use up mental and (sometimes) physical resources, but gaining us nothing in return. Consider the three examples below:

Joy joined Malcolm Ellis to help with the administration when his business was just eight months old. Four years later, she is officially Company Secretary, and unofficial 'knower of all things'. Although she has an assistant, Joy is unwilling to delegate as things are never done quite as she would do them. She is so overworked that she regularly does not leave until seven or eight at night and always takes work home at the weekend. She knows every aspect of the business, a role she enjoys; but she finds it frustrating that everyone comes to her for advice and information and, although they are enthusiastic, no one works as hard as her. Increasingly, she is feeling the pressure and resents her long hours and the way everyone leans on her.

Karen is worried about the possibility of being made redundant at some point during the year. She spends many evenings thinking about being unemployed, what will happen to the family without her earnings, the difficulty of getting another job, and imagining what it would feel like to be called in to her manager's office for the dreaded dismissal.

Laura has not been to see her brother since they argued; she feels responsible for the fight and bitterly regrets the things she said. She has gone over and over the argument in her mind, reliving it and feeling the anger on the one hand, but regretting the harsh way in which she made her point.

Joy is caught in the 'indispensable trap'. She has let herself become indispensable to those around her and now resents what she has to do and the pressure it causes. Karen is adding to her stress level by worrying in an unproductive way, using mental energy but achieving nothing. Laura is stressed by guilt, a major problem for those people trying to achieve the impossible and not managing it. Invariably, they feel guilty for the things they fail to do without recognizing all that they do achieve.

The three chapters in this section deal with these three problems in turn.

6

The 'indispensable trap'

It is so easy to get trapped in a cage of others' demands – *and* at the expense of doing what *you* want to do. This is not a problem if you are quite happy with what you are doing, but if you resent the demands made on you by others and the way in which you are taken for granted, you could be in the trap.

Consider the following questions:

- Do you end up cooking/
  ironing/whatever while others
  read the paper or watch
  television?   YES/NO
- Are you the one who
  always agrees to work late or
  through your lunch break?   YES/NO
- Are you the only one who
  can understand/use your systems
  at work, and consequently have
  to answer questions for others?   YES/NO
- Does everyone turn to you
  with their problems, certain in
  the knowledge that you will
  listen and help solve them?   YES/NO
- Are you taken for granted
  by colleagues/friends?   YES/NO

If you have answered 'yes' to any of the above, you have fallen into the 'indispensable trap' in that situation. Note that the word 'indispensable' does not describe you as a person; the trap usually relates to one or two situations or people where you may have a problem.

Some people thrive on being in the trap – but they are seldom doing anyone any favours, least of all themselves. These are the willing martyrs who are happy to be the last one to leave the office, who always volunteer to help, or who turn down offers of help with 'It's OK, I can manage'. There is no problem with being indispensable – provided you are totally happy in that role, and do not begrudge being taken for granted. However, if after a while you are left working late alone, taking on the tasks that no one else wants to do, or preparing a meal and doing the washing-up while everyone else is watching television, and *resenting it*, then you are caught in the 'indispensable trap' and should start looking for a means of escape.

The main feature of the trap is that you are usually the creator of your own problems. For example, if you have always shrugged off offers of help and insisted that you can manage, it is not surprising if the offers have dried up. Similarly, if you have always agreed to work late or take on the unpleasant task, others come to assume that not only will you do it, but that you do not mind. The good news is that if you can recognize how you came to fall into the trap, you have taken the first step in accepting responsibility for your own actions and planning your escape.

The other important aspect of the trap is that in trying to help others, you may actually cause them problems; consider the two situations below:

Simon left home at the age of 20 and moved into a shared flat. He has endured the teasing of his flatmates because he couldn't iron a shirt, peel a potato, or sort out his washing before the visit to the launderette. He is the son of an 'indispensable mother'.

Bessie, at 78, spends all day watching television. She has come to rely on her daughter's twice-daily visits to make her flasks of tea, dinner and sandwiches, do her washing, and so on. There is no medical reason why Bessie could not do these things for herself; she is the mother of an 'indispensable daughter'.

Simon's mother has not done her son any favours by doing everything for him, and Bessie's daughter is not helping her mother by not allowing her to do anything. It is quite possible that *you* have become 'indispensable' – if so, you have a responsibility to change this!

PUTTING IT INTO PERSPECTIVE

Pause to consider when you fall into the 'indispensable trap'. Why are you vulnerable to this trap? In what type of circumstances? How does it make you feel?

Make notes regarding these questions, and others, below:

_____

_____

_____

_____

_____

_____

_____

_____

Take three steps to escape from the trap

As we have seen, too much to do is a pressure that contributes to stress, and the negativity of resenting some of what you do simply adds to the strain. If that resentment causes you to be short-tempered and sarcastic, your relations with those around you are likely to be strained – which adds still more to the pressure. It is important to escape from the trap; below are some general 'keys' to help you, followed by 'positive steps' to help you make specific plans.

STEP ONE

If *you* do not consider yourself and your needs, who do you think will? If you are sending the message that others' needs are more important than yours, who is to blame for other people believing you?

- Next time you find yourself resenting what you 'have' to do, ask yourself: (1) Why have I ended up doing this? (2) What do I need at this moment?

STEP TWO

Having decided what you want and need, it is important to communicate this clearly to those who are taking you for granted. Make sure that your resentment does not show in your voice or manner; keep it warm and positive.

37

- The answer to (2) above will usually be fairly clearly defined – for example, 'I need help with tidying the house'. Sometimes you can take immediate action, so stop dropping hints about how tired you are and ask directly for the help you need. Ignore any surprise shown by those you ask; if everyone is used to you coping without complaint, they are bound to be taken aback if you ask for help. However, when you *do* get the support you need, say thank you with good grace (but don't grovel!).
- Where the answer is not so clearly defined (e.g. 'I need them to stop using me as a fax machine operator just because the machine is by my desk'), you will need to plan a little before acting. Identify what you would prefer people to do and what needs to be done to help them (each person will need to be shown – by sending their own fax while you supervise and guide, and/or given a typed list of instructions to support this). All that remains is to *tell* them.

STEP THREE

Look to the future and identify the situations where you tend to fall into the trap. See if you can understand why you feel obliged to take on everything, and decide whether these reasons are valid.

- Choose one situation where you can see you are at risk of falling into the trap and decide how you will avoid it. Plan what you will say and, if you do not find the words comfortable, practise in front of a mirror so that you are used to hearing yourself saying them.

POSITIVE STEPS FOR PROGRESS

List three occasions when you fall into the 'indispensable trap' (you may find it helps to return to the list of tasks you identified in the first part of Chapter 2). For each one, note your needs in the situation and then plan how you can get out of the trap and/or how you can avoid it in the future.

It may help you to look at each task you resent and decide:

- Should I be involved in this at all?
- Should I hand over total responsibility to someone else?
- Should I ask someone to help on occasions?

THE 'INDISPENSABLE TRAP'

1 _____

My needs: _____

_____

_____

_____

I can get out of the trap and/or avoid it by: _____

_____

_____

_____

_____

_____

2 _____

My needs: _____

_____

_____

_____

I can get out of the trap and/or avoid it by: _____

_____

_____

_____

_____

3 _____

My needs: _____

_____

_____

_____

I can get out of the trap and/or avoid it by: _____

_____

_____

_____

_____

_____

7

Don't worry

What is worry?

Worry is generally related to things that *might* happen – it is fear of the unknown or the unwanted. For example:

- David's worry about his dentist appointment is based on the fear that he may need to have a tooth extracted.

- Shula's worry about her new manager is based on the fear that they may not get on and that she might lose her job.

- Andy's worry about the presentation he is making to a client tomorrow is based on the fear that he may forget what he is saying, or not be able to answer questions put to him.

- Samantha's worry about leaving on time is based on the concern that she may not get the supermarket shopping done in time to collect her daughter from school – who would then be left standing alone at the gates.

Worry and stress are often mentioned in the same breath, but they are in fact very different. For example, imagine that you drive into the back of another car on your way to work. You will probably suffer *specific stress* as your adrenaline immediately surges. You will then suffer *general stress* as you fit in the aggravation of calling the recovery service, ringing the office to say you will be late, arranging for insurance forms to be sent, the repairs done, etc. In contrast, *worry* describes your feeling of dread at having to tell your partner about the accident when you get home.

Worry is both a waste of time and a major contributor to stress. However, it is very easy to say 'don't worry', but much harder to prevent ourselves from doing so. If you feel that worry is adding to your stress level or wasting your time and energy, invest a little time and thought in sorting your worries out.

In the first column in Figure 11, list the *type* of things that worry you. These are those situations that do any, or all, of the following to you:

- Cause you to lie awake at night going over and over them in your mind.

41

- Come to mind when you least expect them.
- Make your stomach 'sink'.
- Keep coming up in conversation, but do not get resolved.

Remember that these should be general things, not specifics (e.g. major events in my children's lives, *not* my son's driving test).

When you have listed the types of things you worry about, identify what fear it is that causes the worry (be honest!).

Type of worry	Based on fear that
e.g. A major event in my children's lives.	*They will be hurt by failure. A failure will reflect badly on me/their upbringing.*

Figure 11

Look over your responses and see whether there is a pattern in the type of things that worry you. If so, note it below:

I tend to worry about things that: _____

_____

_____

_____

_____

If you feel that worry is adding to your stress level, now is the time to take positive action.

KEEP A 'WORRY-PAD'

A 'worry-pad' is a small notebook or pad. Keep it with you at all times, and every time you find yourself worrying about something, note it down and then put it out of your mind. As often as you find it necessary, go over your worries in a 'panic period'.

SCHEDULE A 'PANIC PERIOD'

Put aside half an hour or so, or as often as you need it, to think through these worries. If you are a great worrier, you may need to build a 'panic period' into every day. For other people, once a week may well be enough.

At the start of your half-hour, find somewhere where you won't be interrupted, either by people or the telephone ringing. Take your list of worries, and for each one:

- Define exactly what it is you are worried about.
- Consider the worst that could possibly happen.
- Say what you would do about it if this were to happen (a specific action plan).
- Say if there is anything positive you can do to prevent it happening. If so, plan to do it; if not . . .
- Don't waste time worrying about a 'what if . . .'; wait until it happens.
- Look at the positive side, what is the best possible outcome? What can you do to make this more likely?

EXERCISE

Try a 'panic period'

Jot down below the things that are currently worrying you. If you need more space, just carry on with a separate piece of paper.

Schedule a 'panic period' to go through the questions, noting your thoughts. At the end, decide what (if anything) you can do about each worry.

43

Worry no. 1 _____

_____

_____

What is the worst that is likely to happen? _____

_____

_____

What can you do to prevent this 'worst' from happening? _____

_____

_____

If the worst does happen, what will/can you do? _____

_____

_____

What is the best possible outcome? _____

_____

_____

What can you do to increase the chance of this happening? _____

_____

_____

Worry no. 2 _____

_____

_____

What is the worst that is likely to happen? _____

_____

_____

What can you do to prevent this 'worst' from happening? _____

_____

_____

If the worst does happen, what will/can you do? _____

_____

_____

What is the best possible outcome? _____

_____

_____

What can you do to increase the chance of this happening? _____

_____

_____

You may find that it helps to put your worries into order of importance, or even some sort of time scale, but only do this if you feel it is useful.

It is often interesting to use a small hardback notebook so that you can look back over the things that worried you a year or so ago; this can help you identify what *was* worth worrying about and what *wasn't* – a useful lesson for the present and the future.

POSITIVE STEPS FOR PROGRESS

Now that you have tried the format in this exercise, go back over it and, if necessary, change it to suit you, the particular things that worry you, and so on. Devise your own questions and issues to consider, and note them for future use.

8
Guilt

There are two types of guilt that affect our stress level.

The first is the uncomfortable feeling that results from doing something that we perceive as wrong; this is our conscience doing its bit to keep our behaviour to a standard we are comfortable with.

> Doreen is feeling guilty because she was short-tempered with a customer today. She had been trying to catch up with the paperwork when a man asked her advice; however, he had little idea what he actually wanted and kept changing his mind. Doreen feels that her tone of voice gave away her impatience.

> Sanjay is feeling guilty because he has borrowed a book from a friend and now cannot find it. He has not been asked to return it yet, but should have done so before now – and he knows it will be difficult, if not impossible, to get hold of another copy.

These are examples of rational guilt.

The second type of guilt, irrational guilt, is less specific but more dangerous.

> Kelly feels guilty because she has not spent as much on her son's birthday present as she did on her daughter's. Money is tight and, despite the fact that she has bought the present he wanted, and was relieved to find that it was inexpensive, she has the uncomfortable feeling that she is not treating her children fairly.

> Tom is feeling guilty because he has not been to see his mother recently. Because she lives a long way away, he can only see her at occasions such as Christmas and Easter; although Tom rings her regularly, he feels that – as her only child – he should be doing more.

> Frankie finds it a struggle to combine working with her responsibilities as a single parent. It is her daughter's class assembly tomorrow, and Frankie is feeling guilty that she cannot take time off to attend as she has used up all her leave and flexitime. She also feels guilty that she always

46

leaves work exactly on time (to meet her daughter from school) when the others often stay on a little late. This feeling of guilt often leads to her working through her lunch hour without a break.

Dominic feels bad that his low salary and lack of savings means that he cannot buy the type of house that his wife lived in before they married, and that their car is the oldest one parked outside the school gates.

Irrational guilt is the result of pressure to achieve or conform to certain standards. Sometimes, though, this pressure comes from others:

Charley's mother no longer drives, and Charley usually takes her to the supermarket on a Saturday afternoon. On the occasions when this is not possible, her mother makes comments along the lines of 'After all the driving about I did for you when you were young . . .' or 'Your lot just don't have the time for the likes of me . . .' Although Charley knows her mother can, and does, take the bus to the shops, she still feels guilty.

Occasionally the feeling of guilt comes from our awkwardness at the difficulties of others:

Barbara feels guilty about her happy marriage and family life whenever she speaks to her sister, Ann, who is recovering from yet another broken relationship.

Scenarios like these do not really involve guilt so much as discomfort. Generally, there is nothing we can do to improve the situation – Barbara can do little to help Ann form more satisfactory relationships. In these circumstances we should accept our good fortune, but not gloat over it. Occasionally, the person we feel awkward about feels the same about us, as the following example shows!

Barbara's sister (Ann, in the example above) feels guilty because Barbara and her husband Pete have so little money and three small children. Ann's job is well paid, her company car is large, and she has a lovely flat in the best part of town.

More commonly, the pressure comes from within ourselves, as in the examples of Kelly, Tom, Frankie and Dominic above. These four were all setting unrealistic standards for themselves and then feeling guilty at their failure to achieve these. Kelly's son was delighted with his birthday present, Tom's mother is touched by how regularly he keeps in touch, Frankie's daughter recognizes that her mother cannot always attend school functions (although she always plays games with her in the evening), and Dominic's wife adores him and is unconcerned with material possessions.

EXERCISE

What do you feel guilty about?

List below anything that you feel guilty about. It may be difficult to put into precise words because guilt is often non-specific, and also because you may find it an uncomfortable subject to think about. However, be as specific as you can. If it helps, think of one aspect of your life at a time (e.g. work, children, family, etc.).

_____

_____

_____

_____

_____

_____

_____

Now tick the items where you are right to feel guilty (situations like Doreen's and Sanjay's above). These are examples of rational guilt.

Rational guilt

The situations you have ticked are the occasions when you are right to regret what has happened. You have two choices:

1 Face the problem and the person, apologize, and do what is appropriate to make amends. This is usually best when the incident is recent, small and comparatively insignificant; if it is more serious, though, consider whether it is best to own up, or whether doing so will ease *your* guilt but destroy someone else's trust or confidence unnecessarily.

Danielle has just returned to her office, having apologized to her colleague for losing her temper with him earlier. She had not looked forward to the meeting and was relieved that her apology had been accepted and that the matter was closed. She wishes, though, that her short affair with Jack was so easy to put right. Although it ended over two years ago, she still feels guilty, and her stupidity in getting involved often comes to mind. Sometimes she is tempted to own up to her husband; she rationalizes that if she explains how bad she feels about the affair and why it happened, everything will be all right. Logically, though, she knows that this would destroy her husband's trust and gain nothing, and again she resolves to keep quiet and let her discomfort be a reminder not to repeat the mistake.

2 If it is too late to apologize, or not appropriate to do so, then accept that you feel bad (and should do), but try to put the matter to the back of your mind and let the memory slowly fade. When the memory does resurface, push it away again. However, don't forget to plan positively for what you would do in a similar situation next time you face it, so that you don't make the same mistake again.

Irrational guilt

Return to the list of things you feel guilty about and put a cross (x) by the items that involve irrational guilt. These are the ones that are the result of emotional blackmail by others or your own unrealistic standards.

List the three most important things below:

1 _____

2 _____

3 _____

Spend some time thinking *why* you feel guilty. For example, are you comparing yourself to others whose circumstances are different, or with characters in television programmes or advertisements?

Take each of the items and rationalize it. For example:

'I feel guilty because I could not afford to take the family on a foreign holiday this year. I explained the situation and they understood. We had some inexpensive "treats" that everyone enjoyed, and the children loved my being at home for two weeks with the focus on what they wanted to do. No one has complained about staying at home.'

GUILT

I feel/felt guilty because: _____

_____

Rationalization: _____

_____

_____

_____

_____

_____

I feel/felt guilty because: _____

_____

Rationalization: _____

_____

_____

_____

_____

_____

I feel/felt guilty because: _____

_____

Rationalization: _____

_____

_____

_____

_____

_____

It is essential to recognize that irrational guilt is futile, a waste of time and an unnecessary pressure. When you next feel this emotion, think it through, talk to others if need be, and then put it to the back of your mind and keep it there.

PART 3: BUILDING SKILLS

In the Introduction, it was pointed out that the only ways to make sure that stress does not ruin your life is either to reduce the amount of stress you have to deal with, or improve your ability to deal with it.

Now that you have evaluated your current situation and looked towards the future, it is time to look at those 'building skills' that will help you reduce the amount of stress you experience as you do the things you have to do. There are six chapters in Part 3, each of which is designed to help you develop a different aspect of coping. The first chapter looks at how you use your time and how to remove some of the things that waste it. Planning is dealt with in two sections: the first helps you to plan your time by using lists in a proactive way, and the second guides you through a system of planning to help when a major task has to be fitted into the workload.

You will find some help in discovering ways to cut corners where you are putting too much into a task, and one such area is to delegate work. Delegation is not just a 'management task' – we can all do it, at home and at work, if we make a bit of effort. Finally, you will be offered some assistance in saying 'no', so that you can avoid getting involved in things that you would rather keep out of – one sure way of reducing the workload!

9

The most of every minute

There is no way of gaining more time in a day: 24 hours is the maximum available. Likewise, there is no way of 'banking' time – in other words, putting some aside to be drawn out and used on a day when it is needed; we have to use time as we get it.

If a colleague took some money from you and did not give it back, you would face a difficult problem that would need addressing and might have to be reported to a manager. However, if that colleague takes some *time* from you, perhaps by chatting to you, or by regularly asking for your help, you may not even notice. We do not give time the same priority as money, and consequently we can let it drift away as carelessly as dropping £5 notes in the street.

Not having enough time means that most things you do are rushed, done with one eye on the clock. This creates a feeling of pressure, which of course adds to your stress level. There is also the problem that a rushed job is unlikely to be well done and you may have to go back over something to do it properly. Poor use of time is demoralizing – and thus is *another* pressure!

Where does time go?

Before you can do anything to improve your use of time, you need to know where it is going at present. The way to do this is to complete a 'time log'. This is tedious, but it is also the most effective base from which to make improvements. You should keep your time log for around three days – ideally five days. Make as many copies of the log as you need and complete it *as you go along*. Fill in all the columns, noting the activities and interruptions accurately and *honestly* (see Figure 12). Time logs contain the following categories:

Start time: This is the time you started (or resumed) work on *each* task, or the time of each interruption. This will enable you to calculate how long you are spending on particular tasks.
What I am doing: This requires only enough information to remind yourself.
Initiated by: Did *you* decide to do the task, or did you respond to the need or

Daily Time Log   Date: _____

Start time	What I am doing	Initiated by Self Other (who?):	Activity completed:

Figure 12

54

request of someone else? If you are noting an interruption (e.g. a telephone call), leave this blank as it is obviously initiated by the interruptor. The purpose of this column is to give you an idea of how much of your time is managed by you and who is managing the remainder.

Activity completed: Insert tick if you completed the task, or leave it blank if you need to come back to it later. This column will show you where you are wasting time by repeatedly having to return to tasks.

Having completed the time log, you will be encouraged to review your use of time and will also need to refer to it as you work through details of the time-waster section that follows. A few example extracts from time logs are shown in Figures 13, 14 and 15.

Example Time Log

Start time	What I am doing	Initiated by Self Other (who?)	Activity completed
0630	Got up, washed, dressed, etc.	✓	
0650	Mark - breakfast/ lunchboxes	Mark ✓	✓
7.10	Breakfast/tidying kitchen/testing Sarah's spelling	Sarah	✓
7.35	Finished make-up, etc.		✓

Figure 13

55

Example Time Log

Start time	What I am doing	Initiated by Self Other (who?)		Activity completed
0850	Arrived at work, got organized	✓		
	Rang Thripps because delivery not arrived	✓		
0900	Post opening, etc.			
0907	Answered telephone (Mr Brasor)	✓		
0910	Made coffee			
0915	Went to see Jack representation this afternoon			
0935	Drank coffee while reading post		David	
0937	Answered telephone (Thripps)	✓		✓
0940	Coffee/post			
0942	Answered telephone (Sue)	✓		
0944	Answered telephone (Despatch dept)			
0946	Coffee/post			

Figure 14

Example Time Log

Start time	What I am doing	Initiated by Self Other (who?)	Activity completed
6.10	Ate tea		✓
6.30	Planned tomorrow	Andy	✓
6.35	Tel - for Tina		
	Cleared up		✓
6.45	Explained homework to Dan	Dan	
7.00	Ironing	✓	✓
7.10	Find football sock	Dan	
7.12	Ironing		
7.20	Hunt shoelace	Tina	
7.21	Tel - for Tina		
7.30	Hunt shoelace		✓
7.40	Ironing/test Dan tables	Dan	

Figure 15

Review your time log

Only you can decide when your use of time is good, bad, or somewhere in between. Time use is likely to vary according to your mood, the pressures on you, and a variety of other factors. In the following section you will be encouraged to work through some of the common time-wasters and to assess their impact on you. Your time log will help with this. Before you get to these specific aspects, consider the following general points:

- How much of your time do you control (and how often are you at the beck and call of others)?
- To what extent do you allocate your time appropriately to important and trivial tasks?

Amanda is making a cup of coffee, and is boiling the kettle while emptying the washing machine. She is also running a sink of hot water to soak some dishes, and thinking about what to have for dinner. She is combining trivial tasks.

Next door, Kate is helping her son to learn how to multiply fractions. She is sitting down, totally focused on this important task, and is giving it 100 per cent.

Both Amanda and Kate are using their time effectively, by combining the trivial and focusing on the important.

- In general terms, how much of your time is spent doing what you should be doing and that which you want to do? It is easy to get involved in things that are nothing to do with you; this presents no problem if you are doing it because it is what *you* want. However, if you are getting involved where you should not be, and do not *want* to be, then there is a problem to be addressed.

If saving time were easy, you would already have achieved it and would not be reading this book. Saving large chunks of time is almost impossible unless you give up a particular activity and, even then, the hour or so a week you might save often dribbles away in a few minutes here and there.

The key to saving time is to stop trying to achieve the impossible, or at least the unlikely, and instead to concentrate on saving just a few minutes. To return to the earlier analogy with money: you may not be able to put £100 aside, but if you drop one or two 20p pieces into a pot every time you look into your purse, it is surprising how much money accumulates.

If you can save three or four minutes throughout during the day, your time will accumulate in the same way as savings. If you control where your time goes, you can utilize these savings.

The time-wasters

Below are some of the most common time-wasters. Read through them and consider their presence in your day. For each one that you have to contend with, consider how you can reduce its impact or even dispose of it altogether. The time-wasters are not in any particular order.

BUMBLE BEE

A bumble bee alights at each flower, pauses for a short while and moves on, tempted by the next bloom. He never 'finishes' the flower, always leaving some pollen on it.

Emma works freelance, from home, and is very busy this week. Typically this coincides with demands from the family, with her daughter playing in a netball match, three potential buyers coming to view the house, her husband's difficult week at work, and friends coming to stay at the weekend. Emma is organized and has lists and notes to remind her of what to do, when, and so on. On Tuesday morning she settles down to write a proposal that is already a day or so late. She is halfway through when she remembers she promised to iron her daughter's sports shirt. She does so while thinking about the detail of the proposal, but soon starts writing a mental list of all the things to put into the report she is writing for another client. The postman arrives, bringing two orders, and a large cheque that is outstanding. She enters up the accounts and paying-in book and starts to parcel up the orders. The telephone rings with another order, so she moves on to this, printing the invoice and packing the goods. She remembers that the iron is still on and decides to finish the ironing while it is hot. She pauses to prepare her shopping list as she thinks of necessities and to put a brochure in an envelope in response to an enquiry. By the end of the morning, everything is underway, but nothing has been completed.

Return to your time log and identify every occasion when you stopped during something that was not finished. Note some examples below:

Task I left: **How long would it have taken to complete it?**

_____

_____

_____

_____

_____

_____

Often, it would not take long to finish a task, or at least get to a sensible place to break off. If you have to stop because of an interruption, ensure that you go back to the task, rather than starting something else. By completing the things you start, you will benefit in two ways:

1 A sense of achievement because things are done and not outstanding.
2 A time saving because you do not keep wasting time getting back into a particular task.

Help yourself
- Next time you find yourself leaving a task unfinished, force yourself back to complete it, and then reward yourself when you have.
- If you are interrupted (e.g. by the telephone) always ask yourself when the interruption is finished what you were doing before and, wherever possible, return to it.
- Next time you have to leave a task, ask yourself how long it will take to complete it. It is often not a great deal of time, and that realization can encourage you to finish it off. If you cannot complete it, knowing how much time is involved will help you re-schedule it.

CONFOUNDED BY CLUTTER

Ralph is looking for the letter to his mother that he had started the night before. He had seen it in the morning and knows he could finish it before his wife gets home, if only he could find it. He rummages through the piles of paper on the desk and kitchen worktop, and through the newspapers by the chair where he had written the first part the night before. He eventually finds it, caught on the back of a paperclip holding some newspaper clippings, just as his wife's key turns in the lock.

Return to your time log and see whether you wasted time looking for things, or in wading through clutter to sort out the bits you needed:

I wasted_____ minutes looking for_____

I wasted_____ minutes looking for_____

I wasted_____ minutes looking for_____

I wasted_____ minutes looking for_____

Help yourself
- Adults tend to lean towards being naturally tidy or naturally untidy, and you simply cannot turn yourself from one into the other overnight.

However, you can make small improvements and, once you find you are on top of the chaos, the order brings its own rewards.

- Look at the clutter and divide it into sections (e.g. papers, old magazines, clothes needing repairs, etc.). For each section, decide where it would be best kept and how it could be kept tidy.
- Look at alternatives for trays, folders, files, noticeboard, and so on.
- Look at your untidiness and consider what systems would help you to become organized; plan to implement them, one at a time, and see how they help. You may have to modify them a couple of times to make them work for you.
- Try to avoid 'squirrelling' – hoarding things that might come in useful one day. If you have piles of magazines waiting to be read or to have recipes removed from them, put two in your car to read next time you have to wait for someone. Throw away anything that has been hanging around for more than three or four months. Similarly, give/throw away clothes you have not worn for a couple of years; and put away/give away cassettes or CDs that you never listen to.
- Appoint yourself as a 'clutter consultant'. If you were being paid to sort out the mess as a third party, what would you recommend? If you cannot do this for yourself, appoint a competent friend!

'DEAD TIME'

Fiona hung around outside the supermarket, cursing it for not opening until nine. Later, her feelings were much the same as she waited at the school for her son to return from his field trip. That evening, she spent an hour chatting to other mothers while her daughter's dance class was in progress. Fiona lived just too far away to drive home, and resented the hour she had to wait each Tuesday.

Return to your time log and identify the 'dead time' in your day:

_____

_____

_____

_____

_____

_____

Help yourself

Use the 'dead time' productively:

- Use the time actively, e.g. write out your shopping list while waiting for the shop to open, have a file of papers with you to read, keep those magazine articles that you must get around to in the car.
- If you use a scheduled task list (see Chapter 10), always have it with you. You can use the time to get organized or plan some future activity.
- If you are stuck somewhere with nothing to do, accept that there is nothing that can be done. Instead, consciously relax, enjoy the view, or listen to the radio.
- If you have a regular 'dead time', use this as a period to unwind.

INTERRUPTIONS

Amin's desk is by the corridor in the open-plan office, and it seems that everyone stops to talk to him. He has got his space well arranged to suit himself, and has a couple of low chairs and a coffee table which he uses for informal meetings; the trouble is, though, colleagues tend to sit there and chat. He also has the problem that because he faces the main door, visitors tend to approach him first – despite the fact that the secretary is nearer (but facing away).

Return to your time log and identify the interruptions (both by telephone and by people). Divide them into:

- *Time-takers* – e.g. if you are paid to answer telephone queries, you cannot treat them as a waste of time; however, you need to streamline them to reduce the amount of time they take.
- *Time-wasters* – e.g. if you get telephone calls because the switchboard doesn't know who else to put them through to, then they are time-wasters.

Time-takers: **Time-wasters:**

_____   _____

_____   _____

_____   _____

_____   _____

_____   _____

Help yourself
Deal with time-takers by:

- Getting down to business quickly, e.g. replacing 'Hello, Judi, how are you?' with 'Hello, Judi, what can I do for you?'
- Stating a time limit at the outset, e.g. 'Have you got a minute?' Reply: 'I've got around three, is that enough or shall I call you this afternoon?'
- Bringing conversations to a close by summarizing the discussion or action to be taken and confirming with the other person.
- Supporting your closing tone with non-verbal behaviour, e.g. collecting papers together, closing a file, etc.
- Visiting others rather than inviting them to your office. That way, you have control over when you leave.

Deal with time-wasters by:

- Investing time in preventing them, e.g. briefing the switchboard on who to put calls through to.
- Trying to avoid getting involved in the first place. It is easier to say you have not got time at the outset, rather than when the person is halfway through the detail.
- Not looking up, unless someone arrives at your desk:
    Eye contact ➡ smile ➡ greeting ➡ conversation = time-waster
- Learning to say 'no' (see Chapter 14).

NOTHING TO DO WITH YOU

Norah had just agreed to complete the pile of letters before 4.00 when Tom came in to ask for her help. She felt sorry for him because his secretary was off sick, and then agreed to help him with some typing. At 12.30, Nicky looked in: she was having a hard time at home, and Norah agreed to meet her at the canteen half an hour later. Having spent half an hour helping another secretary to do a mail merge and another quarter-hour proof-reading a colleague's figures, Norah spent the rest of the afternoon typing. At 4.45, she gave up the idea of going to the supermarket on the way home – she would have to stay late again.

Return to your time log and look for any examples of getting involved in things that are nothing to do with you. Obviously it would be a sad world if you never helped anyone, but make sure that you are not giving priority to favours to the detriment of your own workload and stress level.

Help yourself

- When asked to help, consider whether you have the time and the inclination.
- Make sure that *you* call on others for help when you need it. Don't operate the double standard of being available to others, but soldiering on alone with your own work.
- Learn to say 'no' (see Chapter 14) so that you can do so if necessary. Make it clear that you are refusing the *request* and not the *person* and, wherever possible, suggest alternatives.

PERFECTIONISM

Susie finally printed off the final draft of the report after a day's work on it; she had spent the last hour trying to get the printer to print the appropriate shades, working from the colour chart she had. She only hoped the printers would make as much effort when it was handed over to them. Susie felt it was a shame they would have to re-set it and not use her carefully presented draft.

Return to your time log and identify where you put in too much time or effort, like Susie spending time on making a perfect draft.

I wasted time on perfection by: _____

_____

_____

_____

_____

Help yourself

- As you start a task, assess the quality that is required from you.
- Accept that while excellence is generally desirable, *sometimes* a lower standard in less time is preferable.

POOR PLANNING

Gary rushed out of the office at 12.30 and strode along the high street to get his suit from the dry cleaners. He was just approaching the building when he remembered that he had not got his cheque-book and was out of cash. Cursing, he walked back along the high street to his bank, where there was the usual queue for the cash machine. He wished it was 8.30 in the morning, when he usually walked past, as then there was never anyone at the machine. He walked back up the street and collected his suit and then called in to the sandwich bar. Since it was now one o'clock, his favourite sandwich fillings had gone and he had to have egg salad, which he ate on the way back to the office. Halfway through the afternoon he remembered that he had to buy a bottle of wine to take out with him that evening, so he left the office at 5.20 to rush up to the off-licence next door to the dry cleaners.

Return to your time log and consider how much time you waste by duplicating tasks, journeys, etc. For example, do you make extra visits to the supermarket on the way home because you did not plan your list properly when you did the weekly shop? Do you have to ring people to whom you have just spoken because of something you forgot to say? Add up the amount of time wasted by lack of planning – what else could you have done in that time?

I could have saved myself time if I had thought before I: _____

_____

_____

_____

_____

Help yourself
- Get in the habit of stopping to think before moving, ringing people, etc. Make a list of all the things you need to do before doing something or speaking to others.
- Use a task list, noting all the things you have to do, and then highlight the priorities.
- Where you have several things to achieve, list them, and then decide on the most time-efficient order of doing them.
(See Chapters 10 and 11.)

PROCRASTINATION

Geoffrey picked up the letter from Joan Target and reached for the phone to ring her. He anticipated the argument that was likely and put the phone down, deciding to ring her after he had drunk his coffee. He picked up the Cooper project file and read the papers from which he would have to write his report. He couldn't see an obvious starting point, so he put the file down and reached for his dictaphone and the pile of letters to be answered. He put the difficult ones aside and started on the remainder.

Return to your time log and look for those occasions when you put something off. You possibly lost three minutes, perhaps as much as ten minutes, by remembering that you had to do it, worrying about it, thinking about it, and putting it back on the pile of things to be done. You probably could have done the task in the time you took in putting it off.

Examples of procrastination:

Help yourself
- Tasks that you put off tend to fall into two categories: those that you have to do eventually, and those that you will never get around to.
- Identify things that you will not get around to in the foreseeable future, and either decide not to do them or decide how you can get them done without doing them yourself.
- List the things that you have to get around to eventually. What is it that is stopping you (be honest!)? How long will the task take? Can you do it now? If it will take too long, break it into smaller chunks, making sure that the first three are so small as to be laughably easy. With this approach, you will find that jobs often take far less time and stress than anticipated and, even if the worst does happen, it was only what you were expecting!
- Stop saying 'I'll just . . .' as a way of avoiding getting down to something. It is easy to be tempted by a usually undesirable task when you are trying to get on with something difficult.
- If you find yourself thinking 'I must do that later', change your thoughts to 'I'll just do this now'. Or, if you are already in the middle of something, 'I'll do it as soon as I have finished this'.

WASTING PRIME TIME

Serena works from home in the morning. She has most energy early in the day and as soon as her family has left she tidies up the house and generally gets the chores out of the way. Once a week she drops the children at school and goes straight to the supermarket as soon as it opens. When everything is organized, she often feels a bit weary and makes a cup of coffee and reads the newspaper before settling down to start the three hours' work that she needs to do each day. The work is detailed and requires concentration, so Serena often gets up for more coffee, but, even so, she seldom finishes it before she leaves for the shift she works in the afternoon. She walks home with the children at five o'clock, and when everyone is settled for the evening she returns to finish her 'morning job'.

Return to your time log and consider when is your prime time. This is the period, usually between one and four hours, when you feel most energetic. It might be first thing in the morning, or you may be one of those people who does not come alive until after coffee-time. Some people get a second burst of energy later in the day or in the early evening. Conversely, you should also consider your 'flat spot': that time in the day when your eyelids are prone to droop and your energy is limited.

My prime time is: _____

Secondary prime time: _____

My flat spot tends to be around: _____

Help yourself
- Use your prime time for the tasks that demand the most mental energy, things that are complicated and demanding. This time is also good for jobs like filing where accuracy is important, but the work is boring. They will pass much quicker if done when your energy level is high.
- When you hit a flat spot, try to find a task that involves talking to people; human contact will distract you from tiredness. Movement will also help as it will raise your heart beat and allow your body to take in more oxygen. Visit another floor using the stairs rather than the lift, or try to find something to do that requires a five-minute walk outside. Just walk along the corridor and back if that is all that is available to you, but make sure that you walk with a purpose and move your whole body – do not shuffle along. Avoid eating chocolate for energy; it will boost your energy initially, but this reaction will be short-lived as the body recognizes a sugar 'overload' and your digestive system works to restore the balance.
- If you tend to get a secondary flat spot when you return home from work in the evening, you will probably benefit more from a short rest and a cup of tea rather than the exercising mentioned above.

- Plan for and manage your prime time and flat spots positively.

Tasks to fit into my prime time: _____

_____

_____

_____

_____

How I can do this: _____

_____

_____

_____

Best way for me to avoid a flat spot: _____

_____

_____

_____

_____

THE WRONG TIME/THE WRONG PLACE

Cathy wanted to ask her manager's advice about an important meeting that was coming up. She had left two messages for him and had called in at his office, but he was not there. She was just leaving to go out for lunch when she saw him in the car park, climbing into his car. She ran across and explained her problem. He did not have much time as he was already late for a meeting, but gave her some brief advice. However, she later realized that she had forgotten to raise a couple of points and could not remember what had been said on a third. It was not the place for a meeting.

Return to your time log and look for examples of taking action at the wrong time or in the wrong place. It may not necessarily involve others; for example, did you try to do some complicated task in a noisy environment or when you were tired and irritable? Did you try to talk to someone about a private matter in a public place? Below, note any examples you find, together with a note of when or where you should have done the task or spoken to the person.

What I did: **What I should have done**:

_____   _____

_____   _____

_____   _____

_____   _____

Help yourself

Before doing something, ask yourself these questions:

- Do I have to do this *now*?
- Is there a better time and/or place?
- If so, how am I going to arrange that better time or place?

THE WRONG FACE

Arthur was feeling depressed and had done so for some time. Ever since the company had been taken over there had been rumours of redundancies, and Arthur was concerned that at 52 he would be a prime target. He had long wanted to get out of the warehouse and into a less physical job, but was unwilling to ask in case he found himself out of work. Arthur spent all his lunch breaks complaining to any colleagues who would listen, he took the problem home and discussed it endlessly with his wife, he asked the management team secretaries what was happening and moaned to them, but he did *not* ask his own manager – who would have been able to put Arthur's mind at rest. Fifteen minutes with his manager would have saved hours of conversation with everyone else – a waste of everyone's time.

Return to your time log. Do not waste your time, and others', by talking to the wrong people, or perhaps by not talking to the right ones. See if there are any examples in your log and then decide who you should be talking to.

Who I talked to/why: **Who I should have talked to**:

_____   _____

_____   _____

_____   _____

_____   _____

_____   _____

Help yourself

- Next time you hear yourself complaining, ask yourself who is the best person to help you/give you the information you need.
- Decide how you will ask for that help/information.
- Arrange to meet them.
- Ask them.

Look over your responses to the different sections concerning common time-wasters and, for each one that applied to you, plan the first two steps you can take to reduce or remove them. Make sure that your plans are realistic – it is better to achieve a little, than fail to achieve a lot.

POSITIVE STEPS FOR PROGRESS

Bumble bee _____

_____

_____

_____

Confounded by clutter _____

_____

_____

_____

'Dead time' _____

_____

_____

_____

Interruptions _____

_____

_____

_____

THE MOST OF EVERY MINUTE

Nothing to do with you _____

_____

_____

_____

Perfectionism _____

_____

_____

_____

Poor planning _____

_____

_____

_____

Procrastination _____

_____

_____

_____

Wasting prime time _____

_____

_____

_____

The wrong time/the wrong place _____

_____

_____

_____

The wrong face _____

_____

_____

_____

71

10

Using a scheduled task list

Almost every self-help book on any subject relating to time and self-management will suggest writing lists to help you remember and organize everything. This is undoubtedly a good idea, but if you are stressed because of the pressure of trying to fit everything in to a long list of tasks, it can only offer minimal help – and may even *add* to the pressure. A task list can also waste your time and cause you problems with prioritizing:

Wasting time through:	Problems with prioritizing:
• Re-writing the items you have not yet completed on a new list	• The tendency to do the first important (or interesting) thing you come to
• Searching through the list for the thing that you should do next	• Items that are together on your list tend to remain together when prioritizing, often irrationally

However, this is not to say that you should abandon the idea of writing lists altogether; rather, that you should take a more structured approach to doing so.

One way of making a list more useful is to schedule it – in other words, spread the list over a period of time rather than have a long list that covers several days. This does not take any longer – in fact, it is quicker when you consider the problems above.

A scheduled task list

A normal task list is a piece of paper that includes all the tasks you need to do. As you are told/decide to do something, you add it to the bottom of the list. The list is therefore in the order of identifying the tasks to be done. However, a scheduled task list works on a different basis.

Although you may have many roles (e.g. wife, mother, child, sister, secretary, friend), you are only one person. This means that the tasks you undertake in each role need to be combined at the planning stage, just as they are when they are done.

A scheduled task list works on the following premise:

If you are regularly under time pressure you are unlikely to do a task until it *has* to be done. Whether it is tidying the workplace before a senior management visit, or cleaning out the goldfish, there will always be a greater priority until the day of the visit or the point where the goldfish is making windows in the slime on its tank.

On this basis, there is therefore little point in having a task on your list if you know it will not be done for another few days. A scheduled task list focuses on when tasks have to be done, rather than on when you decided/were told to do them.

A scheduled task list runs over a number of days, with items only entered on the day they need to be done. It can be combined with other reminders – for example, a supermarket list, things to do when next in town, a book you want to get from the library. If you suddenly find yourself in town unexpectedly, you can be sure that you have your list of things to buy and do. Similarly, if you leave work a little early you can call in to the supermarket with your list in your hand. You can use it to keep notes of things to tell someone; and when you next meet, you can be sure that everything has been dealt with.

Should you have some unexpected time, you can always start to tackle the items from tomorrow's list!

EXERCISE

Schedule your task list over the next seven days

Fill in the days of the week in Figure 16, with Day 1 being tomorrow. Spend a few minutes thinking about everything you have to do, people you have to see, things you have to buy, and so on. When can you do each? When is the deadline? List them on the relevant days, taking care *not* to list things that you know you will not do and not to list anything until the day you will do it.

Using a diary

The simplest way to do this is to buy a diary – an A5 or small page-a-day one is the best. Use it as you would any diary: enter the dentist appointments, trips to your family, school events, etc. You can put in work commitments if it suits you to do so (to run work and home together like this should prevent you from arranging a late meeting on a day when you have

73

| Day 1 |
| Day 2 |
| Day 3 |
| Day 4 |
| Day 5 |
| Day 6 |
| Day 7 |

Figure 16

```
24
October


Birthday card to Sarah
5.15 - Jamie to Dentist
Buy salad for supper
Renew work car park permit
Book hotel for 15 November
Note to school for tomorrow          baked beans
Ring Uncle Ned - OK?                 washing powder
Mr Jackson visiting shop floor       mince
Sleeping bags to launderette         local paper
Make/freeze shepherds pie            fish fingers
See Carly                            mayonnaise
Check time film starts               orange juice


              CARLY
              Cover school run?
              Recipe for fish dish
              Phone no for Don


        1    2    3    4    5          Lasagne
  6    7    8    9    10   11   12
  13   14   15   16   17   18   19
  20   21   22   23   24   25   26
  27   28   29   30   31
```

Figure 17   Example page from a diary-based schedule

to be home early for a particular reason).

In addition, though, enter the tasks that you have to do. Although there is nothing to stop you listing when to do the washing or cleaning on a regular basis, this is likely to be rather a waste of paper. However, if something *has* to be done on a particular day (e.g. ironing on Wednesday because of the need to wear a particular shirt on Thursday this week), then put it in. Your diary will thus include:

- One-off appointments.
- Things that have to be done regularly, e.g. a child's swimming lesson.
- Chores that have to be done on a specific day.
- General 'to do' items.

You can also include the shopping list, notes of things to ask friends or family (listed on the day you will see them), and even the meals you plan for your family.

The point is that the task list is flexible, containing everything you need, and you should use it in the most appropriate way for you and your lifestyle. You are unlikely to get it right the first time, but persevere, be flexible, and you will soon have a system that suits you.

Have a look at the example page in Figure 17, and then consider how you could operate a scheduled task list.

11

Engage brain before body

If your days and evenings are already full, just one more thing to do or organize can feel like the final straw. It is obviously easier to fit in a pleasurable addition to your workload, like a holiday, but sometimes even then the hassle of getting everything organized can dull the enjoyment of anticipation.

Preparation for any major event can be off-putting, and it is all too easy to delay making a start and then have to tackle it at the last moment, in a rush, with inevitable mistakes. It is even harder when you are not looking forward to something. The temptation then is to hope that by not thinking about it, this will prevent it from happening.

The way to avoid this is to break the planning and preparation into small tasks and then fit these into your schedule – basically, a little time spent planning saves a lot of time spent panicking. You will find that even a daunting task does not seem as bad when organized in this way.

At its most basic, planning can be done simply by listing the tasks that have to be done. However, this does not help with deciding what to do first. As was mentioned in the last chapter, a list can cause confusion where tasks that happen to be on the list together stay together throughout, often illogically so.

The other disadvantage of a simple list is that we usually think of the easiest, most enjoyable, tasks first and, since they are then at the top of the list, they tend to get done first – again an illogical order and one that leaves the worst aspects till last.

Developing a planning system

For a planning system to work it needs to be:

Random   (The order of ideas at the planning stage do not determine the order of the action)

Flexible   (Can be used for a variety of situations, at work and at home)

Complete   (The task is thought through before work starts)

One popular system of planning that meets these criteria is a 'spidergram'. If you take a look at the example in Figure 18, you can see how it gained its name!

77

STAGE ONE – THINK

Take a piece of paper and draw a circle in the middle; note the task to be planned in the circle.

Now list all the things you have to do around the central circle, grouping them logically. See the example in Figure 18 for a holiday in Tenby. You will see that some of the items are things to do (e.g. book leave) and others are questions to be answered (cattery, or Sue to feed Cassie?).

Figure 18

STAGE TWO – ORGANIZE IDEAS

Decide what must be done first and put the items in order, determining what to do about each.

The list from the example in Figure 18 might look like this:

Check school holiday dates   Book kennel
Book leave – Jim, me   Check clothes: Jim, Me, Kirsty, Charlie
Decide self-catering v B&B   Decide on cattery or whether Sue will
Make booking   feed Cassie

78

Book cattery/ask Sue

Check out hire of roof box

Packing list

Food list

Cancel papers

Cancel milk

You now have two alternatives:

1 You can leave the prioritized ideas in the form above and tick them off when you have done each; this is a *checklist*. If you are going to have packing lists, shopping lists, etc. all relating to this holiday, this might be helpful.
2 You can incorporate the items in your scheduled task list (see Chapter 10).

Choose the system that suits you (and the circumstances).

EXERCISE

Try a 'spidergram'
Imagine that you and four friends have decided to go on a mystery trip to the theatre. It is your turn to arrange the treat, and you are expected to surprise your friends on the night. All the planning is left to you; draw a 'spidergram' for the theatre trip, using Figure 19 as a starting point.

You will find a model answer on page 80 (Figure 20).

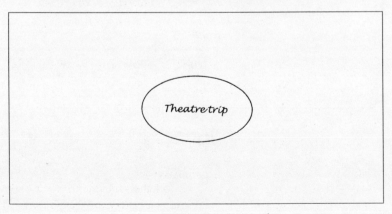

Figure 19

EXERCISE

Now do a 'spidergram' for a real event

Look at what is on your agenda over the next few months (it might help to refer to Chapter 5). Identify something that you need to plan for, either at home or at work, and then draw a 'spidergram' for it.

Identify which items are priorities and plan when you will do these. Draw up a checklist for the event or, if you prefer, incorporate the items into your task list.

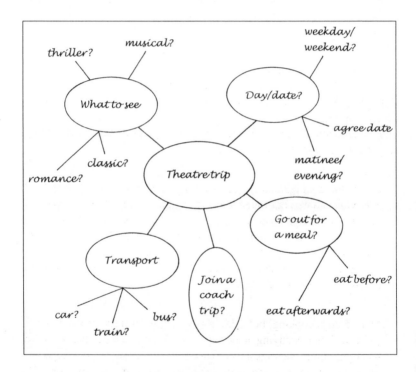

Figure 20

12

Cutting corners

Put time to one side for a moment and think instead of money. Imagine that you have £100, budgeted for as follows:

Rent	£40
Food	£30
Bills	£20
Repayments	£8
Fun	£2

If you want to buy a shirt that you have seen in the sale of a local shop, you will have to reduce your spending on one or more of the items above in order to gain enough money to buy it – assuming, of course, that you have no other income.

You have to take the same attitude to time: you can only gain time by taking it from other activities. For example:

Louise has decided that she is spending too long asleep. She has tried going to bed later, but found that she was so tired that the extra hour of available time was wasted. She is now setting her alarm an hour earlier in the morning, but is finding it increasingly hard to drag herself out of bed. Louise is conscious that although she has the extra time, she is not as effective at work and has made more mistakes with the till receipts that she has to add each day.

Mark enjoys cooking, but seldom has time for it these days. He has a full-time job, is studying at evening classes, and works in the bar of his local pub three evenings a week. He has been living on junk food and pre-prepared meals, and sometimes misses a meal altogether. He noticed that although he was eating less, he was spending more, and he was more conscious of a feeling of stress than a feeling of well-being. Having made a conscious effort to eat one good, if simple, meal every two days, he is already feeling better and is going to return to eating a decent meal every day. He is finding he is gaining time through increased efficiency, rather than losing it on cooking.

Damian is newly married and so busy at work that he has given up his weekly game of football. Although it was his choice, he is increasingly resentful and tends to take this out on his wife. She is actively encouraging him to return to the game, rightly feeling that escape from the pressure, combined with the physical activity, was giving him an escape from the stress he feels at work.

So what can you do?

Rather than trying to save large blocks of time on essentials like eating and sleeping, have a go at saving a few minutes here and there by cutting out non-essentials and by delegating tasks to other people.

The three characters below could save themselves some time by cutting corners:

Petra hates ironing, but has never thought much about it; she simply irons everything as her mother used to do. By not ironing underwear, shirts that will only be worn underneath a sweater, etc., she will save about 15 minutes each time she irons.

Alison does her housework every Monday, a habit she fell into when the children were first at nursery school. Now she works in the afternoon, but continues with the Monday clean-up, following her usual routine of dusting, vacuuming, polishing, sheet-changing, etc. She rather resents the time it takes, particularly since she often has to vacuum again before the weekend to make the house look good for visitors. By cleaning only when necessary, she could have an extra 20 minutes a week, possibly more.

Yvonne is a secretary who hates to make mistakes, and so spends a considerable amount of time proof-reading first drafts of documents and making them look professional before her manager sees them. Her effort is usually wasted because so much of it is changed when he gets to see it. She would save 10–15 minutes a day by accepting that perfect is not *always* best.

These examples all illustrate the 'watch the pennies and the pounds will watch themselves' approach to using your time effectively!

The major barrier to saving time through cutting corners is the pressure to get things right. In fact, this is often a pressure that we put on to ourselves, and it is only us who can remove it. In business and at home, it is *sometimes* better to be 90 per cent right and 100 per cent on time, rather than 100 per cent right and miss the deadline or hold others up. This is not to say that it is acceptable to be careless or sloppy; indeed, in some jobs (such as pharmacy) perfection is more important than time taken. Generally, though, it is the difference between being good enough and spending time you don't have on perfection:

	100 per cent	**Good enough**
Petra:	Visible items should be ironed	Non-visible items don't matter
Alison:	Dirty surfaces need to be cleaned	Clean surfaces don't
Yvonne:	Final copies need to be perfect	Draft copies don't

Let go, live a little!

Sometimes we strive for perfection for our own sake, for pride in a job well done. In other cases, we do it for others – but sometimes perfection is not always what others want; in fact, it *seldom* is. Your efforts can in fact be an irritant to those who you are trying to please. Just consider the situations below:

Binda spends a great deal of time and effort in keeping the house clean and tidy, producing excellent meals, etc. Her husband would rather she sat down with him occasionally or had time to go for walks with the family.

Karen spends a considerable amount of time and money on workbooks to help her seven-year-old with his maths. However, he wants her to play snakes and ladders with him.

Vera puts hours of time into checking the figures she produces every fortnight. Her manager would rather have the figures quicker, but unchecked (they are automatically checked anyway).

Consider what others actually want from you and, more importantly, what you want for yourself. If it involves letting go a bit, do so – live a little!

$$\boxed{\textit{EXERCISE}}$$

Look back at Chapters 2 and 9. Then turn to Figure 21.

In column one of Figure 21

In the first column, list the groups of tasks you do (e.g. report writing, typing, phone calls, shopping, washing, ironing). Choose the ones that you like least and/or take most time.

In column two of Figure 21

Imagine the worst. If you were hospitalized for three months and unable to do anything much for *another* three, what would happen to each of the items on the list? Note this in the second column. Your responses are likely to range from 'wouldn't get done', 'wouldn't get done as often', 'Andy would do it, although not very well', 'Barbara would be able to take over', to 'Charley would do it, but differently', etc.

In column three of Figure 21

Learn a few lessons from column two. For instance, would it matter if some items did not get ironed? Are there tasks you could do less often but would

Task	What would happen?	What lessons can I learn?

Figure 21

notice little difference in? Are there occasions when you should drop your standards? To whom can you delegate? Are there different ways of doing the things you do?

Remember that you are not trying to save enormous amounts of time – it only takes ten blocks of three minutes to give you half an hour.

You do not necessarily have to make these changes to everything you do, or for all of the time. If you prefer, save cutting corners for when you are under pressure.

Choose the three easiest 'corners to cut' and list them below, together with a reminder as to what you are going to do to save a few minutes. Once you have implemented these changes, you can identify another three 'corners' to work on.

1 _____

_____

_____

_____

2 _____

_____

_____

_____

3 _____

_____

_____

_____

13

Delegation

Delegation is a word that is usually applied to a management technique. However, it is equally applicable in any role, and also in a home or social situation.

Delegation involves giving someone a task and the support they need to complete it successfully. You may have to equip them with the skills before they can undertake the work – an investment in time that will save you hours in the long run.

Abdication, though, is the more common alternative; this is where the task is simply passed on to someone else and they are left to get on with it. Not surprisingly, the end result is often not what was required and both parties feel let down.

Three 'good' reasons not to bother

We come up with many reasons for not delegating tasks. The three most common ones are:

- 'It's quicker to do it myself.'
- 'He might get it wrong.'
- 'I've tried it before – it didn't work.'

If you take these reasons to their logical conclusion, though, the arguments don't hold up so well.

'IT'S QUICKER TO DO IT MYSELF'
Of course it is; you have the skill and experience. However, if you invest the time to teach someone else to do it, you will recoup the time when they have learnt. You will also have one less thing to worry about.

When Jackie returned to full-time work, it became necessary for her husband to load the dishwasher. She explained briefly how everything was arranged and which programme to use, but he spent so long fiddling about that she felt like doing it herself. However, she explained *why* things were sorted in the particular way, and the difference between the programmes and so on. Jackie stood beside him on a couple of occasions while he loaded the machine, and the combination of understanding and confidence meant that he regularly took over the task.

'HE MIGHT GET IT WRONG'

He might, but the person who never makes a mistake has never tried anything new, and good support will reduce the chances of errors. Also, he may approach the task in a way that is different from yours but, provided the outcome is acceptable, this should not matter.

Brian was teaching his son to lay the table. Brian always put everything on the table and then went around laying up each place. Jake, his son, preferred to go around and around, first with knives, then with forks, and so on. Brian kept trying to 'correct' this until he realized that provided the table was ready for the meal, how it was done didn't matter.

'I'VE TRIED IT BEFORE – IT DIDN'T WORK'

People do not, as a rule, get things wrong intentionally. By identifying why a mistake was made and then tackling the cause, you can often prevent it from happening again.

Frances wanted her daughter to iron her own shirts. The last time she tried to delegate, she did so by hinting at what she wanted done, and then eventually demanding action when her subtlety was ignored. This resulted in tears and arguments. On this occasion, Frances explained what she wanted and why, and offered to show her daughter what was involved. With this approach, she found her much more willing to help.

The *unspoken* reasons for delegating are often the more truthful ones:

- 'It will reduce my control.'
- 'I won't be essential.'

Beware of the 'indispensable trap'!

Starting to delegate: part I

Decide what you would like to delegate and to whom. This can either be at home or at work:

I would like to delegate _____ to _____

I would like to delegate _____ to _____

I would like to delegate _____ to _____

Before you go ahead, read through the guidelines below and plan how you will delegate these tasks.

DELEGATE IT

Define it   Be clear in your own mind exactly what you are delegating, what is involved, how much should be done, etc. – in other words, the parameters of the task.

Discuss it   Explain what you want and why. Concentrate on the outcome rather than the way in which the task should be approached.

Teach it   Explain what is to be achieved and by when. Make sure that the person knows what they are doing by watching them and answering questions, but not by doing it for them. The important thing is that they feel confident and able.

Watch it   Agree how and when you will check that all is going well and then monitor as agreed.

Reward it   The reward may be specific, or it can simply be thanks and an acknowledgement of the effort put in.

This simple process works whether the task is important or mundane, large or small, although obviously the stages will be more involved for a large, important task.

Starting to delegate: part II

Return to the tasks and people involved, and plan how you can adopt the above approach to each.

Delegate _____ to _____

I want them to: _____

I will explain/teach it by: _____

_____

I could reward them by: _____

Delegate _____ to _____

I want them to: _____

I will explain/teach it by: _____

_____

I could reward them by: _____

Delegate _____ to _____

I want them to: _____

I will explain/teach it by: _____

_____

I could reward them by: _____ to _____

Where your delegation is unsuccessful, spend some time thinking why. The most common reasons for failure are insufficient instruction, lack of confidence on the part of the person being delegated to, or lack of willingness. If at first you don't succeed, withdraw, re-plan, and delegate again!

14

Just say 'no'!

If the pressure of too much to do is causing you stress, then you have to learn to say 'no' to some things. Many people find saying 'no' difficult, if not impossible. This is generally because of a fear of seeming unhelpful or rude, and/or not wanting to upset someone. However, it can also cause you problems if you fear being seen as not able to cope when others around you apparently are.

Our discomfort with saying 'no' often means that when we try to do so, we say it awkwardly, often burying it in apologies and justifications – just look at Lizzie's efforts to avoid having to work late:

'I'm so sorry, I don't think I can stay on tonight. Any other night and I would have been able to, but I must get away on time this evening. Is it going to give you a huge problem? Oh dear, I ought to get away because it is my day for the school run. I'll tell you what, I can stay on for 20 minutes.'

Sometimes it seems that our mind is desperately saying 'no', but our mouth is saying 'I don't really think I can'. Therefore our attempts to refuse are not noticed or are ignored, and we end up doing what we have been trying to avoid.

The most common reason for this failure is a difficulty in saying the actual word 'no'; look at the exchanges below where Henry is saying 'no' (or thinks he is) to a variety of friends and colleagues:

Tony: 'Can you join the quiz team on Friday?'
Henry: 'I don't think so, but I'll see what Ann thinks.'
        Tony is left with the impression that Henry would convince Ann that it was a good idea.

Laura: 'Henry, can you attend the case conference meeting next week in my place?'
Henry: 'It's rather difficult, I've got a lot on at the moment.'
        Henry has left himself open to being pushed into going by Laura.

Andy: 'Henry, I need to bring the deadline for the sales report forward to Thursday, OK?'

Henry: 'I'll do my best, but I am very busy so I can't promise.'
Henry thinks he has left a get-out clause to keep the deadline to Friday, but Andy will be expecting the sales report on Thursday.

Henry's problem is that he is avoiding saying 'no', which leaves the other person with the expectation that he will say 'yes' – in other words, he will do what is requested of him. This will inevitably lead to misunderstandings and resentment in both parties and add to the stress that Henry is feeling.

When to say 'yes'; when to say 'no'

When someone asks you to do something, you have five choices:

1 SAY: 'yes'.
    DO: as asked.
    This approach is fine where you are clear about what you are being asked to do and are happy to oblige; ensure that deadlines and detail are clear. For example:

   'Lucy, can you stay for an extra half-hour to complete this tonight?'
   'Yes, that's no problem, I can stay until 6.15 if necessary.'

2 SAY: 'yes, if you . . .'
    DO: as asked.
    Again, this approach works provided that you are happy to help and that the other person agrees to your negotiation:

   'Sonia, could you attend the team meeting in my place?'
   'Yes, provided you can cover Adrian and my phones.'

3 SAY: 'yes'.
    DO: nothing.
    This approach is based on the fact that it is less trouble to say 'yes' to something and then never get around to it, than to say 'no' in the first place and risk an argument. Although it has little to recommend it as an approach, it may work with the aggressive person who demands things without thinking through whether they are needed, and then forgets

91

about them when the next problem comes along (usually within a couple of hours). If you are tempted to try this, think carefully about whether the action/information really is necessary, in which case you can use one of the two methods above. Remember, though, that you are generally letting someone down by not doing as you have said, and an awkward situation may arise; it is better to get things out in the open and say 'no' at the outset.

4 SAY: 'no'.
DO: as asked.
This has a very negative effect on your self-esteem. Each time that you try to refuse a request, you somehow seem to end up doing what the other person wanted anyway. The most common reasons for this are:

- You were bullied into agreeing.
- You tried to say 'no' to something that you could be made to do (legitimately).
- Your refusal was not clearly heard (see Henry's examples above).

It is the last of the reasons above that is the most common. Make sure that you are not saying 'no' out of habit when you know that you will do as asked anyway. In this situation, save the 'no' for when you really mean it and will stick to it, and use 'Yes, if you . . .' instead. If you find that you are giving in under pressure, read through the section on saying the word 'no' (5 below) and look for some books or classes on assertiveness to help you develop this skill.

5 SAY: 'no'.
DO NOT DO: what was asked.
Saying 'no' clearly and politely will in fact cause fewer problems than saying 'yes' and then resenting it, or trying to say 'no' and not getting the point across (as Henry did earlier). Although some people may be surprised when you first try it, you will find that they accept what you say when they see that you mean it, particularly if you refuse with warmth (see below).

Alternatives 1, 2 and 5 are positive and effective; 3 and 4 are to be avoided!

Saying 'no' and being heard

The first stage in saying 'no' and being heard is to be clear about what you are refusing. For instance, are you refusing to do something completely:

'No, I'm not able to take over the sales returns.'

Or are you refusing to do it at this time or in a particular way:

'No, I'm not able to take over the sales returns this month.'

It can be difficult to be clear about this when under pressure and faced with the question, 'Can you do this?' It is tempting to say 'no' – when in fact you would be willing and able to help if it could be left with you to be done later.

Consider the examples below. These show the difference between saying 'no', and saying 'not at the moment/in this format'. Note that the latter is, in fact, 'yes, if . . .' By turning it round, you avoid a 'no' that is really a 'yes' and so present yourself in a far more positive light.

Note that the examples are *not* two ways of saying the same thing; they depend on what it is you are willing and able to do.

Request	'No'	'Not at this time/ in this format'
'Can you type this?'	'No, I must get this report finished.'	'Yes, it will be done by eleven tomorrow morning.'
'Would you be able to join the committee?	'No, I have too much on my plate at the moment.'	'I can't join the committee, but I will be happy to help on the day.'
'Can you ring Andrew and tell him?'	'No, that should come directly from you.'	'I'll ring him when I have finished this.'
'Can you help with this homework?'	'No, you are meant to do that one unaided.'	'I will give you a hand after supper.'

| 'Could you stay on to get that finished tonight?' | 'No, I have to be away on time this evening.' | 'I can't stay tonight, but I can come in earlier tomorrow.' |
| 'Can you iron my blue shirt for tomorrow?' | 'No, you are old enough to do that yourself.' | 'If you'll clear up supper, that will free me to iron the shirt.' |

The three-stage approach to saying 'no'

STAGE 1: BE CLEAR ABOUT WHAT IS BEING ASKED

Make sure that you know exactly what it is that is being asked of you. Some people tell you clearly what they want; others are vague about detail so that you are not sure whether you want to say 'no' or not. Some people ask in an aggressive manner, either bossing you about or simply assuming that you will do as they wish. Look at these variations on the same request:

- 'Have you got a moment – I know it is a bit of a cheek, but could you possibly whizz these around? I wouldn't normally ask, but I have got so much on and I'm getting further and further behind. Do say if it's too much trouble . . .'

- 'I want this on everybody's desk by three o'clock this afternoon. It's essential that they all get it and read it.'

- 'Hi, I've left a report on your desk to be circulated to each member of the department.'

If you bypass the style of asking and concentrate on the message, you will be able to evaluate quickly what is being asked. Working it out in this way also means that you will be able to respond to what is being asked rather than to any negative tone that may be used:

- 'Please could you circulate . . .'

You may need to ask for more information, and you should do this before you respond. For example:

- 'Are you free on Wednesday?'
  'What is it that you need me for?'

STAGE 2: DECIDE WHAT YOU WANT TO DO

Your choices are to say 'yes', say 'yes if/later', or to say 'no'. Decide which one is appropriate.

Since it is saying 'no' that is difficult, and it is that which we are looking at, we'll assume that this is what you want to say.

STAGE 3: SAY 'NO'

There are four clear guidelines for saying 'no':

1 Get the body language and voice tone right. Make sure that you look at the person as you say 'no' and keep your expression friendly, but without an irrelevant smile.

2 Keep words to the minimum, and do not give a series of excuses and justifications – you will be weakening your case, not strengthening it. Give a reason if you want to, but make sure it is genuine and stick to it.

3 Refuse the request, not the person. Avoid statements like 'I can't do that for you' (when you mean 'I can't do that today'). Concentrate on what is being asked, not the person who is asking for it.

4 Say 'no'. Anything other than the word 'no' is likely to be taken as 'maybe', which becomes 'possibly', which becomes 'probably', which becomes 'yes'! Make sure you use phrases like:

- 'No, I can't do that today.'
- 'No, I'd rather stay at home tonight.'
- 'No, I can't help; I've too much on this week.'
- 'I've helped with four already, so this time it has to be "no".'

'SO SORRY'

There is little wrong with saying 'sorry' in place of 'regret', particularly since most people find that saying 'regret' sounds stilted:

'I regret I can't help with that' – 'I'm sorry I can't help with that.'

However, make sure that the voice tone is that which you would use for the word 'regret', and that it does not become an apology for something you are entitled to say.

If you suffer from 'sorryitis' (symptoms include apologizing to people who bump into you, and for things that are not your fault), practise the discipline of *not* saying the word. You will be pleasantly surprised that its loss has little dramatic effect on others' treatment of you.

EXERCISE

Have a go at 'no'

Think of three examples of the type of requests that are made to you, particularly those where you find it difficult to say 'no'. For each one, write down the words you could use to refuse and then practise saying them aloud. It is important that you get used to hearing yourself say the word. Think about your voice tone and body language at this stage.

Make sure you are clear about whether you are saying 'no' (that you do not want to do it at all) or saying 'yes, if . . .' (when you are saying 'not at this time'). For the purpose of this exercise, concentrate on the occasions when you want to say 'no'. As soon as you are reasonably competent, use one of these refusals when the opportunity presents itself.

1 What will be asked of me: _____

   I can refuse by saying: _____

   _____

   _____

   _____

2 What will be asked of me: _____

   I can refuse by saying: _____

   _____

   _____

   _____

3 What will be asked of me: _____

   I can refuse by saying: _____

   _____

   _____

   _____

When you have a busy lifestyle, looking after yourself is often one of the first luxuries to go. However, this is a short-sighted policy. Just as it makes sense to maintain a car if you rely upon it, it is sensible to look after your physical and mental health in order to increase your ability to withstand life's pressures. So looking after yourself is not a luxury – it is an essential!

To continue with the analogy of a car: just as your vehicle has a body and an engine, you have a body and a mind and, in both cases, the two need to be maintained in order to get reliable and long service.

Care of your mind and psyche involves finding the rest and recuperation that is right for you. Look at the different needs of the individuals below:

Sally-Ann works long hours, which often include weekends. Her job involves travel around the country, and on her nights at home she is often working. Although she plays badminton at the local club, this is irregular and her few days off are usually spent painting her house. Sally-Ann's salvation, however, is three weeks' holiday a year, usually in a far-off exotic land, much of which is spent comatose on the beach. This break, and the anticipation of it, are enough to sustain her.

Gerald reckons he works an average sort of week, and adds to his earnings through occasional work at his local pub. He also visits his disabled mother daily for a few minutes. Gerald and his family have a couple of weeks away each year, and he takes some time off during the children's school holidays. Gerald finds he can cope, provided he has 20 minutes a day to spend on himself. Sometimes he goes for a walk; sometimes he sits still, not allowing himself to think of anything – just to listen and observe. He then feels refreshed enough to continue with his work.

Laura works at her desk all day, answering customer complaints. She relaxes by attending a weekly car maintenance class, which she finds refreshing because it is completely different from her normal life.

Jenny loves to lose herself in a book, and sets aside half an hour a day to read.

Looking after your body does not need to cost money, take hours, or involve lycra leotards! As you will see in Chapter 15, you can exercise at no financial cost, you can combine exercise with your daily routine, and you can wear whatever is appropriate to you. Have a look at the approach in the following chapter, and then plan how you can increase your stamina by increasing your fitness.

15
Fitting in fitness

You would have to have spent the last few years under the duvet not to have been aware of the importance of fitness!

Fitness is essential to breaking the stress cycle. It helps to shed the energy stored by our bodies in response to stress, and to protect us from stress-related illnesses. Exercise also causes the release of endorphins into the body, which generates a feeling of well-being.

Exercise and sport develops stamina, strength and suppleness. Although all three are important, it is stamina that is of most relevance to stress. Activities such as walking, jogging or swimming develop heart and lung capacity and give you the endurance to work at a higher metabolic rate. It has been shown that two or three 20-minute sessions of exercise a week will benefit you both physically and mentally.

This is all very well in theory, as many broken New Year's resolutions testify. In reality, though, exercise can seem a chore, or a luxury that gets crowded out of a busy week, particularly if sports or organized classes do not appeal to you. Therefore if you are to improve your fitness, you need to find an approach that suits you and can be fitted into your crowded day.

Making a gentle start

If you resolve to do three exercise classes a week, or undertake a major change such as cycling to work *every* day, and then find that you cannot keep it up once the initial impetus has worn off, consider starting at the other end of the spectrum.

STAGE ONE

Set yourself one achievable target for a small burst of energy on one day. For example:

- Tomorrow, use the stairs rather than the lift at least once.
- This week, park in a far corner of the supermarket car park (if you park next to a trolley park, you do not have to walk there and back once you have loaded the car). It does not have to be the farthest corner!
- On your way home from work, walk from one bus-stop further.

- Choose a landmark that is a five- to ten-minute walk away and go there and back at lunch time (much more focused than a general wander).

The important thing about all the ideas above is that they take very little time – you will often arrive before the lift or bus, and will feel more invigorated. By the time you have cruised around a car park looking for a space, and then walked the trolley back to its park at the end of your shopping, you will already have taken longer than parking at a distance.

Think about tomorrow. List every single thing you *could* do to build five minutes of exercise into your day:

Now, from your list, highlight one thing you *will* do, once (e.g. use the stairs to go up and down two flights of stairs). The idea is to do just a little more than you do already – something that feels manageable to you in your current state of fitness/unfitness. Make sure that you do this one thing tomorrow, and then carry on to the next stage the day after.

STAGE TWO
Pick something different from the list to do tomorrow and for the next six days (you can do a different thing each day or repeat the same thing if it is not too boring!). If you want, add in a couple of things from the list. At the end of the week, move on to stage three.

Days 2–7, activity: _____

_____

_____

_____

_____

_____

STAGE THREE

Return to the list of ways to build exercise into your day and consider how you can extend them – for example, by walking for 10–15 minutes to a landmark, or by walking to the post office at lunch time, rather than driving there on your way home. On the plus side, you only have to do an activity three times this week, rather than daily.

Extend activity by: _____

_____

_____

_____

_____

_____

STAGE FOUR

Rather like the previous stage, look at what you are doing and identify ways of extending it, keeping to three occasions this week and extending the time to 20 minutes or so.

Extended or additional activities: _____

_____

_____

_____

_____

_____

STAGE FIVE (if necessary)

As above, but increase the pressure a little so that you are walking rather than wandering (if you are not doing so already).

Build up the pressure a little by: _____

_____

_____

_____

_____

_____

There you are – 20 minutes, three times a week, and quite possibly saving time waiting for buses and driving around car parks; easing stress by not fighting for parking spaces; and improving your effectiveness through an increase in energy. Who knows, you could even try an exercise class now that you have more stamina!

WARNING!

As you start to try a little harder, remember to move at a comfortable pace for the first couple of minutes (to warm up the muscles, particularly if you have been sitting down all morning) and, if you can feel your heart beating as you walk, go slower for the last few minutes to allow your heart rate to return to normal and the muscles to come off 'peak performance'.

16
'Me time'

Compare yourself to a rechargeable battery in a toy train – the type that you can put into the charging unit every so often for a top-up, but periodically needs to be completely discharged and then fully charged.

That full charge can be compared to an annual holiday – a week or two away from it all, doing exactly what you want to do. When you return, you work more efficiently and can keep going for longer – until your battery begins to run down again.

However, the top-up charges tend to get forgotten and we keep going, discharging our battery and working on – like the toy train left running around the track while the owner has gone on to play with something else.

If you don't take the trouble to look after yourself, who will? Most people look forward to their annual holiday as a chance to rest and recharge, but if you are to cope with a pressured lifestyle you also need to build in short periods for these top-up charges.

There are two different types of top-up. Just as holidays can be divided into the annual holiday and occasional shorter breaks, top-ups can be divided into the once- or twice-a-week couple of hours' relaxation and the shorter 10- or 20-minute breaks every few days. Either way, they should be 'me time' – time that you spend on yourself.

An hour out

Consider the following question:

> If your fairy godmother gave you a bonus hour or two, once a week, on the condition that you could use it only on yourself, what would be your top three uses of the time?

1 _____

_____

2 _____

_____

3 _____

_____

Have a look at your wish list. Do your choices have anything in common? For example, are they all related to getting outside, exercise, peace, reading, a hobby?

POSITIVE STEPS FOR PROGRESS

Decide whether you would benefit from a planned hour, on a regular basis, doing the same thing – for example, an exercise class. Alternatively, would you prefer to do a different activity each week – perhaps a walk one weekend, a mid-week visit to the cinema, an hour spent reading a magazine?

Now imagine that your fairy godmother required you to 'book' a certain period each week for your hour out; when would it be? How about putting that hour in your diary now, either as a regular slot or just for the coming week?

A 'holiminute'!

If a holiday is a few days off in the year, a 'holiminute' is a few minutes off in the day!

On the assumption that if you feel stressed enough to be reading this, you are probably on the go for between 10 and 12 hours a day. Try to build in a daily rest period of around 20 minutes. Far from being a waste of time, you will be far more efficient when you start again than if you had worked on through this period.

During your daily 'holiminute', try to do the things that *you* want to do – for example, read the paper that you enjoy, watch your favourite television programme, or listen to the radio station that entertains you. For these few minutes, avoid trying to please anyone other than yourself.

See if you identify with the six daily 'holiminutes' that different members of a team take when they can:

Lisa watches a soap opera every evening before she does anything else.

Paula takes a slightly longer journey home, via a country road which is easier to drive than the roundabouts and traffic-laden route that is more direct.

Martin has a quick shower and changes when he gets home, then lies on the bed and listens to the news.

Alan escapes from the noise of his office and the noise of his family by driving home without the radio playing, just enjoying the silence.

Avis has a 20-minute sleep when she gets home at 2.30 in the afternoon, and then leaves to collect her children from school.

Justina stops the car at a local beauty spot and just stands and looks at the view for five minutes.

POSITIVE STEPS FOR PROGRESS

What three things would be your top choice for a 'holiminute'?

1 _____

_____

2 _____

_____

3 _____

_____

How could you build these into your day?

_____

_____

Getting away from guilt

However much we know it is irrational, it is easy to feel guilty about spending time on ourselves. Doreen, though, got around this one cleverly:

Doreen identified the two tasks that she hated most in her week: ironing and cleaning the bathroom. For every minute she spent on these, she allowed herself the equivalent of 'time out'. Sometimes she used this the same day: 20 minutes doing ironing, 20 minutes reading a magazine. Other weeks she 'banked' the time and saved it up to go and see a film. Either way, she was free of guilt about her time off.

Mark was trying to lose weight. He rewarded every pound lost with half an hour of the lunch break he didn't usually get around to taking.

However, remember that you do not need to feel this guilt. You are not doing anyone any favours if you overdo it and become irritable, or even ill. Just a few minutes a day can be the difference between coping and 'going under'.

PART 5: LOOKING FORWARDS

17
Positive steps for progress

As you have worked through the book, you will have come across the 'positive steps for progress' sections. Hopefully you will have implemented some of the ideas – some successfully, others less so. If you have not achieved as much as you wanted, do not give up. Review what you tried to do, those things you *did* achieve, and what stopped you attaining other goals. The following section will help.

Not-so-positive steps!

If you have tried to implement change and been less successful, do not give up. The most common reasons for failure are:

- You are not committed enough to the idea of change.
- You are too ambitious.
- Your attempt was unrealistic, often because of the needs or views of other people.

If you have another reason, note it here: _____

_____

If you were *not committed* to what you were trying to do, then you were right to abandon it. There is no point in adding to your problems by trying to remove stress simply because you feel you should, or have been told that you ought to.

If you were being *too ambitious*, consider breaking down your target into easy stages. Just as in Chapter 15, Fitting in fitness, you were encouraged to start at the bottom and work up in your exercise goals, adopt the same approach to whatever you are trying to achieve. Set small, attainable targets, and note your success. As soon as you start to slide, ask yourself why and what you can do about it.

I tried to: _____

_____

Three steps to get started now: _____

_____

_____

_____

_____

(add in more steps if necessary)

As I achieve each of these, I will reward myself by either acknowledging to myself my success and taking pride in it, or by:

_____

_____

_____

Repeat the exercise above as often as you need to. If it proves to be quite often, make a concerted effort to aim for smaller, more achievable goals rather than setting yourself up for failure.

Your attempt may have been *unrealistic* for any number of reasons. You may have tried to do too much or at the wrong time. You may also have assumed that others would help you and then discovered that they were unwilling to. If the latter is your problem, you may need to talk to the people concerned and explain to them what you are doing and why.

Thomas was feeling both unfit and stressed, so he designed himself a fitness plan based on Chapter 15 of this book. However, he found it hard to keep to his plan because of the teasing of his colleagues and a few sly comments when he was taking a full hour for lunch (which he was entitled to, but seldom took). When he explained to his colleagues what he was doing, he found they were much more supportive than he expected, and a couple of them even went with him on his walks.

Christina decided that she was in the 'indispensable trap' and that she was going to withdraw from some of the things she had been doing for her family. However, they did not seem to notice, and rather than taking over some of the chores such as clearing the table, they simply left them. Christina complained to a friend, who pointed out that her family had taken her for granted for so long that they probably genuinely did not notice what was happening. After explaining her point of view to them, Christina's family made more effort, and gradually she achieved her goal.

Decide where other people have stopped you from achieving change, and whether they are doing it intentionally or not.

I have been stopped from achieving my goals by:_____

_____

_____

_____

They have stopped me because: _____

_____

_____

I will take the following steps to overcome these problems by:

1 _____

_____

_____

2 _____

_____

_____

3 _____

_____

_____

Next time you are unsuccessful in implementing change, first ask yourself why, and then plan a new approach. Don't just give up!

Your own positive steps

Now is the time for a final look at what you want to do, from today, to reduce your stress level. Take a look back over your plans in the 'positive steps for progress' sections and identify what you want to do next. If you have yet to put *any* plans into action, now is the time; and if you are looking forward to taking the next steps, outline your ideas here.

Make sure that your plans are broken down into realistic stages so that you can achieve them in the short term. Building in a reward will also help – either a tangible one, or simply the acknowledgement to yourself of what you have achieved.

Do remember to take pride when you are successful, and never feel that something is too small to be worthy of note – if you don't take the first step, you can never take the second!

1 I want to: _____

_____

_____

I will achieve this by:

a _____

_____

_____

b _____

_____

_____

c _____

_____

_____

(Make sure that these steps are clearly defined, or you will never know when you have achieved them. For example, 'to use more lists' is not as much help as 'to write a shopping list every week' or 'to write my task list in a book, not on the back of an envelope'.)

I will know I have achieved it when: _____

_____

_____

_____

2 I want to: _____

_____

POSITIVE STEPS FOR PROGRESS

_____

_____

I will achieve this by:

a _____

_____

_____

b _____

_____

_____

c _____

_____

_____

I will know I have achieved it when: _____

_____

_____

_____

3 I want to: _____

_____

_____

_____

I will achieve this by:

a _____

_____

_____

b _____

_____

_____

c _____

_____

_____

I will know I have achieved it when: _____

_____

You can now transfer your plan to a scheduled task list, but don't forget to check up on your progress.

Devise your own rules

Quite apart from making specific plans, you may find it helpful to draw up your own rules – that is, some general principles to help you avoid stress.

Jodi has three rules and sticks to them firmly. They are:
Do not get hassled by things that are nothing to do with me.
Quantify worries and only concern myself with the ones that will definitely happen.
Allow five minutes' thinking time per day.

Thumb back through the book, looking particularly at your various responses, and draw up your own rule-book below:

1 _____

_____

_____

_____

_____

2 _____

_____

_____

_____

_____

3 _____

_____

_____

_____

_____

4 _____

_____

_____

_____

5 _____

_____

_____

_____

_____

Remember, you only live each day once, so make the most of it!